Inspired English Teaching

Also available from Continuum

Getting the Buggers to Write, Sue Cowley
Getting the Buggers to Read, 2nd Edition, Claire Senior
100 + Ideas for Teaching English, Angella Cooze
Resources for Teaching Creative Writing, Johnnie Young

INSPIRED ENGLISH TEACHING

A Practical Guide for Teachers

Keith West

A companion website to accompany this book is available online at: http://education.west.continuumbooks.com

Please visit the link and register with us to receive your password and access these downloadable resources.

If you experience any problems accessing the resources, please contact Continuum at: info@continuumbooks.com

continuum

Continuum International Publishing Group
The Tower Building   80 Maiden Lane
11 York Road   Suite 704
London   New York
SE1 7NX   NY 10038

www.continuumbooks.com

British Library Cataloguing-in-Publication Data

A catalogue record for this book is available from the British Library.

ISBN: 9781441141347 (paperback)

Library of Congress Cataloging-in-Publication Data
West, Keith, 1950–
 Inspired English teaching: a practical guide for trainee and practicing teachers / Keith West.
    p. cm.
 ISBN 978-1-4411-4134-7 (pbk.)
1. English language—Study and teaching—United States. 2. Language arts—United States. 3. English teachers—United States. I. Title.
 LB1631.W22 2010
 428.0071—dc22

                                        2010001029

Typeset by Ben Cracknell Studios
Printed and bound in Great Britain by CPI Antony Rowe Ltd, Chippenham, Wiltshire

Contents

Acknowledgements

This book is dedicated to all the students that I've had the pleasure of teaching over three decades and in six different schools. Without you all, this book would have been impossible. Thanks also to my wife, Ruth, and my grown-up children – Becka, Naomi and Jonathan – for proofreading and commenting upon the material used. My thanks also to Christine Garbutt and Melanie Wilson from Continuum for all the help, advice and support they have given me.

Introduction

This book is not about teaching theory – you will have had plenty of theory elsewhere. Whether you are a newly qualified teacher straight out of university, you have had several years away from teaching the subject or you are a seasoned professional wanting some new ideas – this book will show you how to inspire the students in your classroom. If you are new to teaching, it will give you plenty of material to use in your first few years of teaching. Once you gain the students' trust, they will quickly see you as a teacher who can inspire them. You will make a difference and their grades will improve. Why? Because you have given them relevant material that will engage even the most reluctant of students.

Behaviour management is not easy these days and with English there is a balance because we want our students to open up and engage in speaking activities but we also need them to listen!

I have always believed that English is a subject that stands on its own. Students need to learn how to become good practitioners in the mechanics of their own language, which means they need to inculcate a number of skills so that they can communicate their ideas on paper. It is also desirable that they study and learn to love literature – which includes literature of the present, the past and from other cultures. This means that they are presented with and can digest other ideas. They are then able to become more effective citizens. Students not only need to know how to hold their own in a debate but also alter their ideas in the light of new information. They need to listen and respond to others. English, as I am sure you can see, is really three subjects in one! There is much to teach and this teaching needs to be effective.

The way to manage behaviour in the English classroom is to present students with lessons that are interesting, engaging and appropriate for the group you are teaching. A tall order – but not impossible!

This book is practical and the work examples can be used and applied in the classroom. The first chapter is about body language and voice. This is essential for all English teachers. English teachers, more than most subject teachers, need to put on a performance at times. You need to keep your voice intact.

The following chapter is essentially about becoming a confident teacher and taking charge of your own classroom. Chapter 3 looks at whole-school issues and improving your teaching through relevant assessment and technology.

Chapter 4 looks at how to make the boring bits fun. It is so easy to lose a class by trying to teach the students something you might find easy and exciting – but they don't! Collective groans and yawns often mean that you are heading for discipline problems. I have used example lessons in this chapter that have worked for me. The lessons given should allow students to learn new skills and enjoy what they are learning. If the students enjoy what they are learning, they will remember what they have learned.

Chapter 5 tackles the assessment focus and the example material covers both reading and writing. I have used lessons that will work in the classroom and that will keep the students motivated. The majority of the material included in this chapter and in Chapter 6 have been tried and tested in the classroom, and some of it has been previously published and used in the classroom.

The major part of Chapter 6 is focused on practical work for drama in the English classroom. Many new English teachers are afraid to use drama in English but, if done properly, this can be the most rewarding. I have included pieces on Shakespeare, concentrating on the texts *Romeo and Juliet* and *Macbeth*.

Chapter 7 includes a bank of material that can be used in a variety of lessons and adapted for different ages and abilities. It is material that I have found works well in the English classroom.

The penultimate chapter deals with the new GCSE syllabus and exam practice techniques. I also look at revision and some tasks involving AS and A-level students.

Finally, I have included an answers section because I know, having taught for 30 years, how busy you are – or will be when you arrive in the English classroom!

This practical book will show you how to use the English classroom to your advantage, which will forever benefit the students you teach.

CHAPTER 1

Use your body

Body language

We cannot become inspiring teachers unless our body language is right. More than that, we can use body language to control what happens in the classroom.

We often pass judgement on people without even speaking to them. We reach conclusions about people by observing their body language. We must not make the mistake of assuming that students do not do the same sort of thing – they do!

It is interesting to note that about 80 per cent of our face-to-face communication is carried out non-verbally. We send out signals to students in a number of ways: from the clothes we wear to the smiles and frowns we put on. Do take time to observe people in the staffroom, in your local pub or in a restaurant. You will notice little gestures and habits, such as the way people run their hands through their hair, scratch their ears or purse their lips. It all seems obvious – on the surface! However, if we know why people do these things, we can become more effective communicators. If we can recognize body language, we can improve our performance. Remember, whether we are the sage on the stage or the guide on the side, we are constantly being observed – usually by at least 30 pairs of eyes.

We all have non-verbal skills and if we are able to develop these skills, we can motivate the students we teach. In this chapter you will gain a knowledge and understanding of body language and non-verbal skills that will help you in your classroom teaching. After all, a great English teacher needs to be, among many other things, a great communicator!

The face

There is a familiar phrase used these days: 'grinners are winners'. Unless you present your class with an inane, vacant grin you will find this is true. Your face is a broadcaster to your class. You need to make sure it conveys the right message. In today's classroom, it is a good idea to smile at those you teach when you walk into the room. Your smile conveys confidence and friendship.

It is interesting to note that women smile more than men. Male teachers need to be aware of this fact. I admit I copied a well known politician's smile (Tony Blair). It worked for me!

Basic emotions

There are six basic emotions. All of which are expressed at some time in a classroom. If you can 'read' these basic emotions, you will be able to control your own facial expressions and understand those of the students. These basic emotions are: surprise, fear, sadness, disgust, anger and happiness. For classroom control purposes, we should be aware that we display these emotions and that students pick them up. However we feel, when we are confronted by a new class which may appear hostile, we should remember that 'grinners are winners'.

Surprise

When we are surprised, wrinkles appear on our forehead. Usually, our eyebrows curve and often are raised. Also, our eyes become wider and the whites of our eyes become more pronounced. Our jaw drops slightly and our teeth part.

Fear

Our face expresses fear by tensing the muscles under our eyes. Our mouth opens and our lips draw back. Our eyebrows rise and become drawn together. Wrinkles appear in the middle of our forehead.

Sadness

The inner corners of our eyebrows draw up and our lips quiver. Sometimes, tears fall. Hopefully, this won't happen to us but we should be able to recognize when our students are sad.

Disgust

Our upper lip is raised and our nose usually wrinkles. Our cheek muscles raise and our brow lowers.

Anger
Our eyebrows narrow. Sometimes our eyes appear to be 'popping out of their sockets'. Usually, our lips are closed tightly together and some people's nostrils flare.

Happiness
The corners of our lips are drawn back and raised. Our teeth are usually exposed and wrinkles appear on the outer edges of our eye sockets. We smile!

The signals we send out give a clear message to listeners *before* we utter any words in the classroom.

Controlling the use of these emotions can enable us to control what happens in the classroom. Certainly, as English teachers, it is good to exploit these facial expressions when reading poetry or prose. Good actors exploit facial expressions – why shouldn't we?

Posture

Posture is also important. Our posture can send out positive or negative signals. It can convey to students how attentive we are. If you are slumped in your chair with your shoulders rounded and if your eyes do not remain in contact with your class, what message is that sending to the class? You cannot expect to hold their attention! You will certainly look defeated and your body language will convey a negative attitude to your class. They may subconsciously (or consciously) feel that you do not care or that you are tired and lack energy. Students respond better to teachers who seem full of energy and tireless.

If you cross your arms or legs, you are sending out defensive signals. Other body language signals, such as fidgeting, jiggling money or keys, twiddling thumbs or biting your fingernails can all send the message that you are nervous, weak or insecure. Students will quickly respond accordingly! It is much better to stand up or sit up straight and look at the members of your class with an appropriate expression, which is looking attentive and interested in what they are doing.

Eye movement

Eye movement can indicate a great deal about the person talking or listening. A teacher will look sincere if his/her eyes move upwards. Eyes also move upwards if one is talking about the past. If eyes move from side to side, it indicates that the person is talking about the present or delivering a speech. It is interesting to note that if eyes never move upwards to retrieve information, the likelihood is that the person is making it all up! You can, by focusing on the eyes, tell when a student is likely to be lying.

Be aware that winking usually means complicity. It can also have sexual connotations, so it is best avoided in the classroom.

Excess blinking can give a message of nervousness. Normally, people blink 10–20 times a minute. If you blink too much, students may see you as dishonest or incompetent. If you don't blink much, students will read this as not taking on board what is being said.

Hands

According to scientists, there are more nerves between the brain and the hands than any other part of the body.

If you are calm, confident and self-assured, your hands will move very little. They may hang limply at your sides. A hand held flat, with the palm out, usually suggests 'I don't know'. If hands are quite active, it suggests a teacher is jittery, nervous or uneasy. Clenched hands means a teacher is tense, frustrated or angry. If you are sitting at a desk, your hands should be resting calmly on the top. If you are at the front of the room, facing your class, keep one hand in a pocket or keep it slightly active.

Gesturing to avoid conflict and assert authority

Raise a finger as a sign of warning, to stop students you have noticed doing something wrong. This is better than bellowing out an order that will disturb everyone else in the class and could be challenged.

A raised hand – palm towards the student, like a policeman on traffic duty – suggests 'stop'. This signal can be used if a particular student is asking a multitude of questions, or answering everything, or is speaking out of turn. Face the person concerned, give that person the hand signal and then, if appropriate, face another student who may wish to speak. The first student will get the message that you want him/her to be quiet.

Further hand signals

If a student is speaking and you do not want that person to speak, gain eye contact with him/her and place a finger to your lips, nodding at the person. Or engage the student's attention and use a 'zip closed' action across your lips. The student will soon get the message that you require quiet. Again, much better than shouting across a classroom.

Should you want a student to see you, get that person's attention and beckon with a finger. Should you want a student to move places, signal to the student and signal where you want him/her to move to. You have instructed the student without opening your mouth. That way, you have achieved your desired effect and avoided a verbal conflict. The student has to challenge you first, rather than respond negatively to your verbal instruction. Mounting a challenge is far harder for the individual student to do, especially if you have indicated instructions with a smile on your face.

The voice

I have sat through student auditions for school plays and have sat at the back of classrooms, observing lessons. If I can't clearly hear what is being said, then nobody else can hear! The play or the lesson will fail, even if the content is excellent.

Projection of voice is important. As a teacher, you have to adopt a teaching voice. You need to be sure that everyone in the classroom can hear what is being said. It is obvious – but it does not always happen! It's a good idea to check at the start of every lesson, and during the lesson, that all the students can hear you.

Richard Burton was a great actor. He had a deep, rich voice. He could be heard. Richard was not born with a deep, rich voice; he developed the voice! It is said that he used to climb to the mountain tops near his home in Wales and shout out lines from Shakespeare. The mountains would echo back to him. He kept practising until he felt sure his voice was right. Of course, we haven't all got mountains near us – even if we, as teachers, had the time! However, it is good to practise. I used to speak into a tape recorder and then play back until I felt I had it right.

Finding the right pace is also important. A fast speaker will not be understood, a slow speaker will soon bore students and their attention will wander to more devious things! To get it right, listen to established and successful teachers or public speakers and then practise. Do note how some politicians and effective teachers use the strategic pause. This can be amazingly effective for keeping students guessing and gaining their attention . . . but use it sparingly.

'This is what happened next . . . (strategic pause) . . . the old man shot his suffering dog.'

A question of voice

I have been fortunate in my teaching career in that I can fill my lungs full of air and shout. However, I have mostly done this when demonstrating how a person would behave in a given situation when I have been teaching drama! I have rarely used a loud and powerful voice as a method of control. I honestly believe that in today's classrooms bellowing at students becomes counter-productive. You run the risk of students laughing at you – then what do you do? You are immediately thrown into a possible no-win situation.

Teachers cannot operate without a voice. However, many Postgraduate Certificate of Education (PGCE) students go through courses, at present, without any voice training. Newly qualified young teachers often suffer complete voice loss six or eight weeks into the job.

It has been suggested that actors could help teachers and instruct them on how to use their voices. This is unlikely to work, as the daily voice load of an average teacher is much higher and more varied than an actor's. English teachers, especially, need to use their voices in a variety of different ways – be it reading in different accents or different pitches, or modelling drama-related activities.

Whatever we think about how society has changed, we have to accept that we are living in an increasingly noisy world. The culture that present students are imbibing means they are less practised in focusing on vocal sound than students were even ten years ago. The spoken word is not enough – students require visual clues before a message can be fully grasped. It is not easy to present a message orally and preserve the voice.

The most common problem that teachers with untrained voices experience is a complete loss of voice. This can be due to poor breathing habits. If your breath is consistently taken only into the upper region of the lungs, then you will have voice problems.

Voice training should include relaxation techniques because a tension in the chest and neck can create a lack of support for each breath, which causes a raising of the larynx in the vocal tract. This in turn can cause the teacher to speak on a note above his/her optimum pitch. Speaking above your optimum pitch will soon cause voice problems.

Voice training should include the development of a good posture and will also include a focus on cantering the breath. A good teaching voice should have a firm flow of centred breath, a developed resonance that will allow the voice to be projected without strain or effort, and a pitch range that allows for flexibility to vary the tone.

Following are some suggestions to help you protect and develop your voice:

- Stand and move with your muscles relaxed. Make sure that you have postural alignment, especially of the head, neck and shoulders.
- Try easy breathing. This includes releasing your out-breath slowly and easily. Then comfortably let your in-breath fill the base of your lungs – remembering to expand your lower ribs.
- Try to do the above exercises a few minutes each day. This will allow you to find support and strength in your breath when speaking to your classes.
- Your larynx works best when it is moist. Do drink plenty of water every day, to keep your larynx moist. You actually breathe through your mouth when you speak.
- Make sure that you give your voice a rest at home or at school, should time permit. If your voice does get hoarse, rest it and sip water.
- Remember to breathe slowly and easily. Release your breath easily and let it out slowly. When you are ready, breath in, filling your lower lungs and centre. Repeat three times.

- Avoid harsh or frequent throat-clearing. Again, sip water and avoid clearing your voice.

Correct voice training is important. If you have experienced vocal difficulty, it is worth seeking help. You do not want a voice problem as an English teacher and, as indicated above, most of these problems can be avoided.

There are various voices English teachers can use effectively in different situations. These are as follows.

Giving instructions

As English teachers, we need to give instructions at times. Sometimes the instructions we give might be mundane. You may ask members of the class to get their books out of their bags, or to place essential equipment for the lesson on their desks. However, there are times when you really want students to listen to clear instructions. These could be important, such as how to set out a report or how to work on a non-fiction text. You might instruct students on how to organize themselves into groups for an oral task. Whatever the situation, you need the students to listen in silence. To gain the required silence, you could use the 'traffic signals' approach, where you act as a 'policeman' holding up your hand as if stopping traffic.

Once students are quiet, you need to convey an atmosphere of calm. After all, you are using this opportunity to present them with information. You are telling the students what they have to do. They *need* this information in order to fulfil the task you have set.

Speak slightly louder than you usually would. Make sure that your instructions are clear and precise, and speak slowly – so they can take in the information you are giving out. Speak with authority, give the impression that you know what you are doing and you have worked it all out.

It is a good idea to look serious and keep still. Make sure that you are in the front of the class, in a central position, if your room permits this.

When you have given the students their instructions, check their body language and facial expressions to see if they have understood. Puzzled expressions, the shrugging of shoulders, the odd comments and low-level talking will suggest that the students have not understood! Question one or two students about your instructions. Ask them to paraphrase what you have just told them.

If your instructions have not been understood then repeat them, stopping at various points to see where the problem lies. Keep questioning the students until you are happy that the task in hand has been fully comprehended.

Once the instructions have been understood, you should have a problem-free lesson.

Storytelling

If done correctly, and with fun, storytelling can be a huge asset to a teacher who wishes to make an impact on a class. These days, it cannot be assumed that students have had the experience of sitting beside their mother (or father) and quietly listened while a parent has read stories to them. Some students have claimed that they have never been read to. Yes, they have watched films or parts of films. They have stared at television screens for hours on end and/or played video games. But have they had the experience of listening to stories?

I have seen Year 7 students looking up at me, some of them sucking their thumbs, completely absorbed by a story I am reading. It really is a thrilling experience for an English teacher, when you realize that members of the class are totally 'lost' in a story and that they are journeying with the characters in an imaginary experience.

The wonderful thing about storytelling is that you can use so many 'voices'. You can read in a passionate voice or pretend anger, sadness or happiness. You can use any emotion the book or poem is suggesting to you. The class will 'feel' for the characters.

When reading stories, you have to be an actor. Your pace can be fast or slow or as varied as you like. You can move about – but not too much. You can be as loud as you like or as quiet. Pregnant pauses are effective, if used sparingly.

There are many books that I can recommend that really do work with students. *Buddy*, by Nigel Hinton (1983), is a must for every English stockroom, as is *Tribes* by Catherine Macphail (2004). Try reading the two walk of death scenes from *Tribes*. When reading these pieces, you will have the students hanging on their seats in anticipation. They are there with the protagonists. If the bell goes for break, you stand the risk of missing out on a cup of tea! This book also has humour and does not 'sag', as many possible class readers do. There is a specific section dealing with guidance and work on *Tribes* later in this book.

Try different accents for different characters, too. There is a Scottish journalist, known as Gail, in *Stone Cold*, by Robert Swindells (1995). I 'do' a passable Scottish accent but if students pick up on the fact that 'my' Scottish accent is not like the real thing, I use humour. I shrug my shoulders and say, 'Didn't you know, she had a Welsh mother.' That usually does the trick. Shelter, a character from the same novel, can be read using a clipped Southern English military accent. Whereas Link is from the north, so a 'Bratford' (Bradford) accent will suffice. Robert Swindells is from Bradford, so a Yorkshire accent is what he probably intended for Link. There is also a character from Liverpool and some

Londoners, so there is a variety of accents to exploit in the one book.

Some English teachers are naturally good at picking up accents, some might need to practise. Video-tape or record somebody with a particular accent from a film or a TV drama. Listen to the accent over and over again, and then imitate that particular accent. A Yorkshire man allowed me to record him demonstrating various Yorkshire dialects. The recording came in very handy when I was reading *Kes* (Hines, 1976) to my GCSE class.

If not overdone, students appreciate, and ask for, the books to be read using accents. They can picture the characters more clearly. This helps when it comes to written work, as characters can be distinguished in the students' minds.

Why did John Steinbeck use so many surnames starting with C in *Of Mice and Men* (1937)? My GCSE students were often confused, trying to remember Curley, Candy, Crooks and Carson. Even after writing brief profiles of each character, they never remembered the differences. Even watching the film didn't help. I solved this problem by reading the book to them, using a different American accent for each C character. Candy was read slowly, in a high-pitched, quavery voice – the voice of an old man. I made Crooks speak like an educated black man from the Deep South. I upped the pace for Curley, the boss's son. He also spoke in a slightly high-pitched voice. He was different from Candy in that he spoke fast, like a young man. Carlson spoke in a deeper, grave voice. After all, he shot Candy's suffering dog out of compassion for the dog and his mates . . . the dog stank. He had to come across as thoughtful and serious minded. It worked! They remembered the characters! This approach is worth trying.

The main reason for speaking in different accents and various storytelling voices is for the benefit of the students; never as an ego trip for frustrated or would-be actors! The aim is for the students to remember the storyline and the characters, or to engage with the book being read.

The work faster/work harder voice

This voice is necessary when students are not working hard enough or are becoming disruptive. At the front of the class, it is often a good idea to engage in brief eye contact with the student who is not on task. Once eye contact is engaged, shake your head, showing the student that you disapprove. You can also wag a finger and point to the work or mime 'Come on' or 'Get on with it', thus avoiding verbal confrontation.

If a student still fails to engage with the work, try walking around the room and then stand behind the student, so that he/she is unable to see you but can feel your presence. You can peer over, as if looking at what he/she has (or has not) done. If you feel a need to speak, try some humour. 'My grandmother can work faster than you (pause) and she's been dead for over 20 years' or 'Hope your favourite football team's work rate is better than yours, or they'll get hammered this Saturday.'

Another option is to have a private word with the student concerned. This must be said in a low register. You might say, 'I want this work completed by the end of the lesson, please.' Always appear calm (even if you do not feel so) and polite. If you remain polite, the student is at fault if he/she hurls you a mouth full of abuse. Keep the focus on the work not done and do not make it personal. You would be wrong in saying, 'You're a lazy little so and so, Spriggs.' You might remember teachers saying such things in classrooms when you were a student. This is not the best approach to imitate and you lay yourself open to a mouthful back. This then becomes a conflict situation that you could have avoided.

Never give out threats that you cannot carry out. Avoid saying phrases such as, 'I'll get your mother in and tell her you're a lazy good-for-nothing toe rag.' Threats of that nature are likely to fail. You might get, 'My mum don't care 'bout what I do at school.' And the student might be right!

Do check that the reason the student is not getting on with the work set is because the work is too hard for that student, or that the work is misunderstood. Check that the work set is appropriate and that the student knows exactly what has to be done. Sometimes, students misbehave because they are afraid to admit they are stuck.

Encouraging and discouraging voices

When helping students with their work, use an adult-to-adult voice, while looking mostly at their work. Students can usually tell when they are spoken to in a patronising voice. They do not like it! They like to think that they are grown up, even if they do have some way to go before adulthood happens.

To encourage a class, make sure that you focus on all the students. Do not be tempted to focus on one or two students. Talk in your normal voice and give praise at the end.

Everyone likes praise, it makes us feel good about ourselves. It actually works! People feel happy and uplifted when something good is said about them. Praise individuals early on in the lesson, so you receive the benefit of the 'feel good factor' generated by your praise. It is best not to praise for too long, but do so in short bursts as the lesson progresses.

If students are working on a task, it is a good idea to walk around the class, looking at pieces of work and giving short bursts of praise:

This is coming along nicely, Nadine.

Joel, I like this sentence.

You've some good ideas here, Emma.

Good, Josh. I like the story so far.

Try to praise everyone in the class during a lesson. There is usually something good to say about every individual.

You may need to discourage students from activities you feel are inappropriate.

Remember non-verbal communication? Try it first. However, should you need to talk to a student, (avoid telling off a whole class) talk in a low register and come across as unemotional. Speaking in a monotone can be effective. Speak in a calm, deliberate and slow voice. This actually gives you time to think so that you are able to pick your words with care. Do this as infrequently as possible. If you make a habit of speaking in this way, students will expect it and you will notice the effect will be lost.

Try asking questions that you do not expect the student to answer:

Why are you behaving like this today?

Don't you understand that this kind of behaviour is unacceptable in my classroom?

The emphasis here is talking to the student on a one-to-one basis, when he/she has not responded to other methods. Remember, use the discouraging voice sparingly and do not attack the student's personality. Avoid words such as 'lazy', 'imbecile' and 'stupid', but do explain to the student that the behaviour, action or inaction is unacceptable.

CHAPTER 2

Take charge of your classroom

A question of space

There is a relationship between space allocated in a building and the anticipated time spent in that space. For example, telephone booths have little space because the anticipated amount of time spent in them is thought to be small. Homes for the elderly require about 108 square feet (10 square metres) per person. This is because the elderly are likely to spend most of their time inhabiting that space.

Schools appear to be the exception. The square footage per person in each classroom is small, and when desks, chairs and furniture are added the amount of space is greatly reduced. For an English teacher who wishes to attempt drama in the classroom or who intends to deliver an individual approach to teaching or a more personalized pattern of student interaction, life can be made difficult due to lack of space (future planners need to be aware of this) . . . difficult but not impossible.

For drama in the classroom, it is possible to move desks and chairs to the far end of the classroom. It is a good idea to change available space and keep the classroom flexible, depending upon the activity. For a group debate, for example, desks can be placed in a horseshoe arrangement in the centre of the classroom, with chairs along each side for those not taking part in that particular debate. If students are used to this arrangement, they will come to accept it as the norm. There are advantages in that students come to rely on you, their English teacher, for seating arrangements. They will come to accept that there is not a fixed seating pattern and that they might be working with different groups of people over the course of the academic year. The spin-off for you is that you can manipulate the groups for academic and disciplinary reasons. I will discuss this specifically in a later section.

Teacher space

Obviously, you need personal space at the front of the classroom for presenting lessons, giving instructions and plenary sessions. However, it is good practice to move around the classroom and use the whole of it as your space, depending upon the activity. This gives students the vibes that this is your room, not their room, and that you are allowing them into your space.

The classroom

The classroom is your domain. It reflects your personality. It is true that the students need to perceive your classroom as a safe, calm place – a place where learning is going to happen.

If students walk into a classroom that is strewn with sweet wrappers and there are graffiti scrawled on the desks, with blobs of chewing gum stuck to the seats, the message they will take in is that this teacher allows indiscipline. They will act accordingly! I used to carry a bottle of cleaning powder and a cloth into every classroom! If I caught a student writing on the desk, I used to ask that student to clean up the mess. When a class was ready to leave my room, I used to check that all was in order and that the room was free from any litter they may have dropped. If I did spot any litter I would politely ask if the room could be in the same state as it was when they entered. They soon got the message! Incidentally, if I noticed any litter or graffiti after a class had left the room, I'd clean it myself. I felt it important that the next class started their lesson in a clean environment. This might sound obsessive, but the message sent out to the classes is important – and does help with discipline.

Displays

Students feel positive about a classroom that has their displays on the walls. Displays also celebrate students' achievements.

Displays should be interesting to look at; therefore it is important to make sure that there is a quick turnover of display. Displays of students' work that have become faded and are peeling off the walls is not an incentive to anyone. A student in Year 9 does not want to walk into an English classroom and see work that was done when he/she was in Year 7! It is much better to keep the displays connected to the current learning that is taking place in the classroom.

Students taking the initiative

It is not always possible to find time ourselves. Teachers *are* busy people. I discovered, when I was a head of English, that I needed to delegate. I wish I had discovered that fact in my first years of teaching! I asked some willing students if they would kindly change the display for me. What I discovered is that they did a much better job than I! They formed displays that really did capture other students' attention! Two displays stick out in my mind:

1. I was teaching in a dismal wooden hut and we were working on Shakespeare's *Macbeth* (1951). The Year 10 students had written character studies and I thought that they were good enough to be displayed. The students asked me if they could stay over the lunch break while I marked their books. They could work on the display at the same time. I readily agreed. The students were good artists and they drew trees representing Birnham Wood. They also drew the three witches and a golden crown. They then drew a castle. Inside these drawings were the essays! By the time the colouring was completed, the display looked fantastic. As students entered the classroom, the first thing they did was to look at the display . . . and read the essays.

2. My Year 9 class were writing their own creative poems, having had a visit from a famous poet. I asked for volunteers to work on a display. The volunteers created colourful 'lift-up' flaps which other students needed to lift to read the poems underneath. Two of the flaps did not have a poem underneath. One was left blank and the other had the word 'Boo' written under it. This created great interest for a while, and the poems were read by everyone who entered the room.

Displays as a learning tool

I have always felt it is important to display really good work as exemplar material. For example, if a Year 10 or Year 11 student has written an A* piece of work, it should be photocopied and displayed as exemplar material. This has two purposes:

1. It shows the students that this is the standard of work I expect in my classroom.
2. Other students are able to appreciate what they need to do to gain a top grade.

On very rare occasions, B or C grade candidates will ask why I have awarded them a particular mark, suggesting that they feel their work is worth more. I usually show them the criteria I am working on and point out what they need to do to improve their next essay (I also got into the habit of marking work showing areas for improvement). If a student still challenged a particular mark, I asked that student to read the material on display and then asked him/her to read what he/she had written. Students have, without exception, come away knowing they need to improve. I can then talk through how they can improve!

Seating arrangements

Some writers suggest that seating arrangements can change as your class changes – which means every hour! They claim that it depends upon the activity you are doing with your class. In reality, changing seating arrangements every lesson is not practical, especially if there is not a break between groups. Yes, you can ask a class to alter seating arrangements as students leave, but this can become chaotic and you might like to put your energies into making sure the room is tidy. Sometimes you need to talk with an individual student at the end of a lesson. In fact, I stick with the same arrangement for several lessons.

There are various kinds of seating arrangements, and the way chairs and tables are arranged indicates a number of different approaches and styles. Is one kind of seating arrangement better than another? Probably not! What are the advantages and disadvantages of various seating arrangements? I will look at the alternatives and discuss both the advantages and the disadvantages in the following subsections.

Orderly rows

This method is perceived as the traditional approach. On face value it does appear restrictive. The advantage, though, is that the teacher has a clear view of all the students and the students can see the teacher. The teacher is able to maintain eye contact with all students. This approach usually means that there are aisles in the classroom which the teacher can easily walk up and down. The teacher can then make personal contact with individual students, see what they are doing and stand behind a student if necessary. These days this arrangement is usually favoured by the traditional English teacher or by teachers who are concerned about the behaviour of their classes. It is seen as a safe option. I generally use this method with classes I do not know, at the start of a term. However, I never stay at the front of the class for long but walk down the aisles and around the back. They soon get used to me talking to individuals about their work and talking to groups.

The disadvantage of teaching in rows is that it is harder to involve the whole class. If you adopt this seating arrangement, make sure that everyone is involved in what you are doing; when asking questions, remember to engage students at the back of the class. This can easily be achieved by asking them questions. It is good to move around so that you can see all the students from different angles, making sure they are all on task.

Orderly rows are good for teacher-led lessons.

Horseshoes

I used a variation of the horseshoe for a number of years. I placed the class desks in a horseshoe shape, with two spare desks in the middle of the horseshoe – placed long ways. My own desk was just outside the centre of the horseshoe. Using this method, all students are able to see each other.

The horseshoe arrangement means that the classroom becomes a more intimate place. This gives students more potential for sharing ideas, information and feelings – all so essential for speaking and listening activities, and for debates.

In case you are wondering, the only reason I had two desks in the middle of the horseshoe was that I taught classes of over 30 students in a small room. It is possible to be creative within the classroom, depending upon classroom size and location.

Separate tables

Another arrangement is to seat students in small groups at individual tables. This allows for group work. This arrangement also makes it easier for the teacher to walk around the classroom and check students' work. Also it is easier for the teacher to help individual students when they are having problems with their work.

I have used this seating plan when teaching mixed-ability groups, when different students are working on different tasks or when they are working on the same tasks at different levels. I also use this method when there are teaching assistants (TAs) or learning support assistants (LSAs) working with individual students. When there is a number of students needing help, working in rows or the horseshoe method might prove to be disruptive.

The clear disadvantage of this method is that the teacher cannot see all the students' faces. Also, if a teacher needs to break off the work and explain something to the whole class, it is more difficult using the separate tables plan. However, if you are unfortunate enough to teach in a small room, this arrangement takes up less space.

I have used all three seating arrangements and some hybrids, too. Once I had rows in the middle and far end, and tables down one side. All seating arrangements can work well and it does depend upon the tasks given and your own teaching style. Are you the sage on the stage or the guide on the side? I have been both! I really do not think there is a right or wrong here. If you are expecting your groups to debate their work and to plan a collaborative piece, use separate tables for the lesson. If your classes need to see you and the whiteboard, have them in rows for the lesson. If you want debates, place the tables in a horseshoe formation for that lesson. In this day and age, teachers need to be flexible. It is not always possible to change tables and chairs around very quickly, so organize yourself so that the arrangement can stay for the morning or the day! You may decide to stick to an arrangement for an academic year. Sometimes it is down to whatever works best for you at a particular stage of your career.

Procedures – make your classroom your own

Where the students sit in your classroom is your prerogative and not their right. On the first day of any new academic year it is a good idea to line the students up outside your door. If you have no drawn-up seating plan, allow the boys to enter. They must enter one at a time. They can sit anywhere but they must leave one space either side of them. This means you will have space, boy, space and so on. Then ask the girls to enter and fill any available spaces.

The other idea is to look at your class list and draw up a seating plan before you meet the class. You can then call out the names and ask the students to sit in a place that you have allocated for them. Personally, I would still go for girl, boy, girl. Research has shown that a girl/boy seating arrangement works best for learning and reducing disruption.

Students will quickly ask if they can change places with other students. Do not allow this to happen too early, if at all. If students swap places without asking your permission, deal with the problem immediately. If you fail to do so, you will soon discover that most will have moved within a lesson or two.

Should you use a class list and draw up a seating plan, you will discover that you can learn student names quite quickly. If you have arranged seating on your first meeting with the class, using the space, boy, space method, you will need to ask the students to write their names on a piece of paper. They will need to display their names clearly on their desks. You then write the seating plan down while they are in the room.

It is obviously more efficient to draw up a seating plan before you meet the group. In an ideal world, this would always be possible. In our world, senior management or your head of English might have altered the groups around at the last minute or you did not receive the class lists in time. Both these annoying factors have fallen my way! However, as I have just indicated, there **is** a way around such problems.

The name game

If, like me, you do not remember names easily, then you can play the name game with your classes. I usually play this game two weeks into the term.

Go around the class and tell each student his/her name. If you get the name right, fine. If you get the name wrong, a selected student can start drawing the hangman on the board a single line at a time. See how far you get before the students hang you! Try again at the end of the lesson and so on, until you have all the names firmly in your head!

There is another name game which is a good end-of-term activity. Students write a name on a piece of paper. The name chosen can be someone from the past, present or future. The pieces of paper are handed to you, you shuffle the papers and you write (or type) each name on the board. A chosen student can go first. That student will need to match a student to a name. For example, you choose Steve to have first guess. He might ask Cheryl if she is Michael Jackson. If she answers 'Yes', then she is out and Steve has another guess. If she didn't write Michael Jackson on her piece of paper, she will answer no and then she will have a guess. Each student has a guess until all the students are out, except the one winner!

Teaching styles

There are probably as many different styles as there are teachers. This is because we are all individual. However, you do need to show students that you are in charge. Here are some practical ways of doing this:

- Make sure that you are in the classroom before the students arrive.
- Share your lesson objectives with the students. If they know what you aim to teach them, they will see the relevance of the lesson.
- Move quickly into the lesson so that students do not have time to get bored.
- Make sure that, at the end of the lesson, you review what has been covered. This is sometimes called the plenary session.
- Let the students know what they are aiming for – set the scene for the next few lessons.
- Set up an efficient homework routine. Do check that your homeworks are relevant and allow the students feedback time. Beware, as an English teacher, that your homework tasks are not all written tasks. If they are, you will sink under the burden of marking them all. Do give students reading and research homeworks that you do not have to mark as well as written pieces.

- Use language in a way that builds up a rapport with the students. I have always allowed students to see my human side. They got to like my quirky sense of humour and my corny jokes . . . and the fact that I support Spurs! The jokes, humour and brief talks about football should not take place too soon. Get to know your groups well before you introduce your human side! They must never take the place of a meaty lesson or become an excuse for lack of preparation.

When I do know a group well, I can allow myself to walk around the classroom and whisper in Dave's ear, 'Pity about West Ham last night, Dave. Didn't think they'd get knocked out of the cup so early on!' A week later, when I'm on duty patrolling the corridors, Dave would snigger as he walked by, 'See Spurs did really well on Saturday – losing at home!'

My wife, who has no interest in football whatsoever, has a good rapport in the classroom, mentioning music and exploring students' various music tastes. She engages both boys and girls, as most students like some kind of music.

I have discovered that the most successful lessons are when a teacher insists that students enter the classroom in an orderly way. As soon as they are seated, students automatically have their books out, ready for the lesson. This can be achieved by standing at the door, waiting for the students to enter. The teacher then walks into the middle of the classroom and starts the lesson promptly. The teacher then sets out the lesson objectives in a way that the students can understand and engage with. The way the desks are arranged does not matter. If students know you start a lesson promptly and they feel they are learning something of value, they will be ready for you.

If possible, describe and explain the structure of the whole lesson and give timings for the various tasks students will do during the course of a lesson. If the first activity begins promptly, then you are making explicit demands for a student's attention.

Here is a possible example:

Teacher: This lesson is going to show you how to write from a plan. Your writing will improve a great deal if you do plan your approach and you consider your structure before you write anything. You will end this lesson by writing a factual report.

Look at the handout I have placed on each of your desks. [This handout details a phone message to ambulance drivers, and it is provided online.] Imagine that you are an ambulance driver who has been called to the scene of a road accident. When you arrive this is what you see – read the printed sheet, it tells you what you find as you reach the scene of the accident. You have 3 minutes to read this.

[Students read the handout.]

Teacher: Now, in pairs, role play a conversation over the mobile phone between the ambulance driver and a doctor at the local hospital. What key information needs to be given and in what order? What questions might the doctor ask?

Teacher: You have exactly 5 minutes to complete this task.

[Students work on the role-play activity for 5 minutes.]

Teacher: Right, now I need some feedback. Amanda and Julie, you two looked as if you were working hard. Can you re-enact the role play for us all?

When the role play is complete, ask students what the objective of the lesson was and then ask students to jot down methods they know to communicate their thoughts quickly on paper. They may come up with bullet points, spider diagrams, flow charts or a numbered list.

Students then need to imagine that they are journalists at the scene of the accident.

They should write a quick plan making sure that they have the following details:

- A description of where the accident occurred.
- Witness statements – mentioning what the witnesses saw and what they think happened.
- A statement from the ambulance driver and any policemen on the scene.
- Any details the journalist might have noticed when arriving on the scene of the accident.

Give a 15-minute time allocation for the above activity.

You might want some students to read their plans out to the rest of the class, while some students could give positive comments on how the plans could be improved.

Then ask students to write their report. Remind them that it needs to be logical. They need to know that in a factual report all the relevant facts must be included and any unnecessary information should be left out.

Finally, remind the students what they have learned. They now know how to write a factual report!

This exercise can be done with Years 7–9 students and is good preparation for GCSE tasks to come!

Planning teaching and learning in English: some brief thoughts

Each school will have a particular way of planning teaching and learning. At best, teaching and learning issues are driven and supported by senior management, and each teacher in the school feels that he/she is part of the decision-making process. There is certainly an argument for involving students more closely and making them responsible for their own learning.

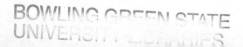

Taking it to the classroom level, I believe students' work improves when they read the teacher's comments on their work and write down *two* targets for improvement. They can then put their targets into action when they next undertake a similar piece of work. This means that the teacher's comments on each piece of work will need to be substantial and the comments should guide students towards improving their own work.

A bad example of a teacher comment would be:

Take care when you punctuate, Fiona.

The above comment is too vague and it does not tell Fiona specifically how to improve.

A better comment would be:

I read your story with interest, Fiona. Although the story was exciting, you need to make sure that each sentence starts with a capital letter and you need a new line for each new speaker.

The above comment shows Fiona exactly what she needs to do. She has two clear targets: to use capital letters at the start of each sentence and to start each new piece of conversation on a new line. In the real world, not all pieces of work need this sort of marking. There is peer marking, which students can undertake for work such as comprehension exercises or spellings. However, if students are asked to write at length, it is a good idea to present them with full comments.

As teachers, we need to plan clear learning intentions through worthwhile teaching activities. We need to make the learning intentions specific to students by telling them at the start of the lesson what we hope they will have achieved by the end of that lesson. For example, you might have a lesson with a Year 7 group on how to vary sentences so that they become more interesting for the reader.

You might plan to show them an example. Tell the students that by changing the order of their sentences, they will make them more varied:

1. If it rains, the match will be cancelled.
2. The match will be cancelled, if it rains.

You could plan that the students write four or five sentences of their own about a forest fire. Then you would ask the students to re-read an essay they have written in the past. Ask them the following:

- What is the balance between speech and narrative in your writing? Should you make any changes to help the reader make better sense of what is going on?

- Underline any words or phrases that give clues to the ending, from the early part of the narrative. Pick out themes from the start of your story that are developed at the later stages of your narrative.
- Underline places in your narrative where you feel more detail (description) is needed.
- Underline any details that have helped to build up the suspense. Where have you offered detailed description and character?

Follow this work through by asking students to work in pairs, seeing where they can improve. Students can then plan and write an essay about a forest fire, improving their writing by putting their own suggestions in place.

The new GCSE curriculum allows for the opportunity to explore creativity, which is now represented more explicitly in the programmes of study. The English curriculum will now allow students to respond creatively in different contexts. I have built in creative examples for you to use in the classroom throughout this book.

CHAPTER 3

Getting to grips with school issues

Literacy as a whole-school issue: an English teacher's input

The secondary school English teacher does not have enough English teaching time to adequately cover all that is required. Literacy needs to be a whole-school issue in that a student's literacy, or lack of it, impacts on all other subjects. For instance, a student might not achieve his/her expected grade in a maths exam because that student might not fully understand the question due to a basic literacy problem. Subjects, other than English, that require a student to write at length (such as history) realize that a student's ability to express him-/herself does count. Of course, reading is about understanding as well as recognizing words.

However, there is a great deal the English teacher can do to help a student improve. Following are a few starting points that can be given out to students, to make them think about their reading.

I can improve my reading by:

- Knowing that reading is difficult to do well and needs to be worked at.
- Looking for the meanings of what I am reading.
- Using my experience of reading other texts to help me understand this text.
- Knowing what the text was written for.
- Realizing that I don't have to read harder books to become a better reader.
- Knowing that I never stop learning how to read lots of different types of texts.

Reading times

In some schools, students are encouraged to read for 15 minutes every day. This can be achieved through form time but, in my experience, that does depend upon the form teacher. Some encourage students to read silently for the allotted time, others let the reading slip in some way.

Some English departments require students of all ages to bring books in from home or from the school or public library. Students are then asked to read quietly for 15 minutes at the start or the end of most English lessons. I encourage this, providing that students are on task and that a box of books is kept in the classroom for those who have 'forgotten' to bring in their reading books. Students also need to keep a log of their reading, which will amount to more than just the blurb at the back of the book.

In my opinion, students should be allowed to read fiction and non-fiction. It does not matter – as long as they are reading!

When a student's reading improves, his/her work improves across the curriculum.

Assessment in English

Following are some thoughts on assessment:

- At best, assessment should enhance the process of student learning.
- The purpose of assessment should be understood by the students.
- Effective feedback should be an essential part of the assessment and learning process.
- Assessment should arise out of the learning objectives set.
- Thinking about assessment actually contributes to good teaching practice.
- Assessment processes should be transparent and encourage active involvement on the part of the student.

At present, assessment practice in English includes coursework, examination, essays, oral assessment and peer assessment.

With KS3 students, I always told my classes what they were being assessed on. If they were writing a creative essay, I would break down the marks as follows:

```
Sustained storyline/plot/character = 10 marks
Punctuation                        =  8 marks
Spelling                           =  2 marks
Total                              = 20 marks
```

If the activity changes, the breakdown of marks can change. The mark scheme is simple, it is easy for all groups to understand and it allows students to realize that an exciting story on its own is not enough. With some groups, I might break down the punctuation expectations into smaller units:

Sustained storyline/plot/character	= 10 marks
Use of capital letters	= 3 marks
Use of full stops	= 3 marks
Use of paragraphs	= 2 marks
Spelling	= 2 marks
Total	= 20 marks

The point is that the assessment chart can change depending upon your assessment focus. Students have the chart in front of them before and while they write, so that they are aware of your marking criteria. It reminds them to use basic punctuation and improves the quality of work that is handed in.

For speaking and listening activities I have used a sheet similar to the one below.

Structure: make sure that your talk has a beginning, a middle and an end. Make sure the start and ending are good. (5 marks)

Interest: make the talk interesting. Make sure that you give the audience as much information as possible. (5 marks)

Volume and clarity: make sure that your audience can hear every word. Check that you speak clearly and not too fast. (5 marks)

Delivery: check that you look at your audience and alter your tone of voice when appropriate. Bring in pictures or use PowerPoint™ to enhance your work. (5 marks)

There are, of course, various ways of assessing these activities and different departments have different marking policies. The point is, whatever method you use, do make sure that the students know what they are being assessed on. Once they do understand the assessment process, their learning will be enhanced because they will know what to aim at.

Effective feedback in terms of marking, with clear targets for improvement are essential. This process allows the students to progress because they have their targets. It also makes you think about the assessment process – what are you giving this lesson for? What are your aims and objectives? What did you expect the students to achieve and how far did their work outcome match up to your expectations?

With GCSE, AS and A-level students, I believe it is essential to give them all a copy of the course syllabus and the assessment criteria. Each student then understands what they need to do to achieve the best grade possible. It is all written down in the syllabus! I then talk to individual students to show them how they can improve. It is also desirable to write full comments at the end of their essays. An example might be:

> This work shows promise, Connor. However, in this essay you needed to mention all the factors that contributed to the death of Romeo and Juliet. Also, please use short quotes to back-up your interesting ideas.

Connor is able to see what he needs to do to gain a higher grade. He can also find two targets from the comments:

1. Mention all relevant facts.
2. Use short supporting quotes.

The following essay that Connor writes on, say, *To Kill a Mocking Bird*, will mention all the relevant points and he will back-up each point using a short quote. Should he fail to do this, he will be reminded about the two targets that he wrote down!

Self-assessment

Most English departments use self-assessment sheets that they hand out to students either at the end of a unit of work or before every half-term.

Self-assessment sheets should include the following:

- How far do I feel I have made progress in English this half-term?
- What are my strengths?
- What are the two areas in which I feel I have made progress?
- What are the two areas where I feel I need to improve?
- My two targets are:

  1.
  2.

Peer assessment

Peer assessment includes oral assessment and reading other students' work to suggest improvements.

Oral assessment

Having given students the criteria for assessment, I then give them a similar sheet to use while they are observing each others' talks.

> Name, structure, interest, volume, clarity
> Structure: Was it well organized and did it start well?
> Interest: Was it interesting and was there enough information?

Volume: Was it clear and loud enough?
Clarity: Did the speaker hold your attention?
(Each of the above sections is to be marked out of five.)

I usually hold a class discussion after the talks. I ask students to say what was good about the talk. I ask them to tell me why they had given a student a particular mark. They can also suggest how a particular student can improve his/her mark.

If students disagree about a particular verdict, it promotes an interesting discussion. They are then encouraged to look at the criteria and come up with a fair mark.

Written assessment

Students can assess each other's writing. I have used the following sheet to help them form a judgement. The sheet can be adapted to the ability of the students.

Name, structure, interest, plot, character
Structure: Does the story make sense? Is it punctuated correctly?
Interest: Is the story interesting?
Plot: Does the plot work?
Character: Do the characters feel real?
(Each of the above sections is to be marked out of five.)

Suggest two targets for improvement when your partner redrafts the essay.

Reports that count

It is possible to write a report about a student that could have come from almost any department. If you covered up the top of some reports and obliterated the words 'English department' could you tell who had sent the report?

Below is an example of such a report:

Ellis has done quite well this term. He achieved a good result in his end of term test but he still needs to improve in some areas.

When I first became a teacher, a fellow teacher had written 'Fair' on a report. The headmaster took him to one side and told him that he must write more about that particular student. He wrote 'Only fair'. We have, thankfully, come a long way since then. However, the above report tells us very little about the student!

Many reports are electronically generated these days, but the English department should have a say as to how report systems are constructed.

It is a good idea for English reports to be split into various sections such as speaking and listening, and reading and writing. Below is a much more useful report about Ellis. His parents will know, after reading the report, how he is doing in English.

Speaking and listening

Ellis is able to talk to his peer group with clarity and purpose. He often chairs group meetings and initiates conversation in pair work.

Reading

Ellis is able to read and comprehend a range of complex texts.

Writing

Although Ellis is able to write at length, he will need to make progress spelling difficult words. He also needs to improve the variety and structure of his sentences.

Targets

1. To keep a spelling book and learn tricky spellings.
2. To write interesting sentences.

Use of plenary sessions

Plenary sessions are important in that they allow you to see if students did learn something in the lesson you have planned and given. This session also reinforces student learning.

You can start by telling the students what they have learned – sum up the session. When you know the students, you can ask them what they have learned.

Example:

Teacher: Right Obi, in your own words, what have we learned today?

Obi: We learned about abstract nouns, sir. They are about feelings, sir.

Teacher: Good, Obi. Now can anyone give me some examples of abstract nouns?

Obi shows the teacher that he has learned something about abstract nouns. The teacher is now checking that the class can give him some examples. The learning process has been reinforced.

Use of technology – the whiteboard as a learning tool

Most English classes have an interactive whiteboard (IWB) these days. IWBs have a number of special features. Anything a teacher or student writes down can be saved or printed because the board is, in effect, a large computer monitor. The advantages for us English teachers are that we can prepare lessons in advance and then display our lessons on a whiteboard. More advantages are as follows:

- No student needs to ask you what a word means because he/she cannot read your writing. Students asking me to read my writing was a blight in my early years as a teacher. My handwriting became progressively illegible as I wrote on!
- You do not need to write on a board with your back turned on the class. Even if you type, your computer can be to the side, so that you have one eye on your class.
- You are able to show computer-generated images and use programs such as PowerPoint™ and Flash Player. You have the ability to access the internet and project web pages for the class.
- Students can present their class talks, using images projected onto the whiteboard to enhance their talks.
- I find that use of the whiteboard stimulates student interest in a lesson. Highly attractive presentations on a subject are possible, using a combination of text and pictures. For example, I gave a presentation of Victorian England using pictures and texts from a variety of sources. I then followed this up by reading from Charles Dickens' *Great Expectations*. I was also able to show clips from a number of films of *Great Expectations*, which meant that the class and I could have meaningful discussions about different directors' interpretations. I have also done this with *Romeo and Juliet*.
- If students are allowed to access Google, they can find information on most relevant topics. However, it is a good idea to check that they are always on task by expecting a certain amount of work in a certain period of time!
- I am sure that students who type their work hand in better work.
- Student participation can include interactive quizzes and close activities. Students feel empowered and confident if they can come to the front and become proactive. Other students can suggest corrections and improvement to answers written by the class or class members. Boys particularly thrive on this type of competition.

Rewards and sanctions
Rewards
Most schools have reward systems such as giving out 'goods' for work and behaviour. Some schools offer badges, pens and calendars. Schools then hold award evenings or ceremonies for students who gain a certain number of 'goods' in a term or year.

Department rewards

Senior management should make it clear why certain students are gaining rewards. Some schools do this well, some do not. However, it is a good idea for departments to devise their own rewards for students. These are effective in developing a department ethos and in rewarding good work and progress.

One reward that appears to work is that of awarding a certificate every Friday, to the two students in each class who deserve it for that week.

On Friday morning, every English teacher will give the head of English the name of two students. One student will have produced the best piece of work in that class during that particular week. The other student will have made the most progress.

The trick is not to give the same two names every week. You will find that the reward works best when the students' perception is that anyone within the class can win the reward, providing that they put in the appropriate effort.

The head of English will then spend a small amount of time during the morning filling in the students' names. Once the certificates are filled in, they can be sent to the appropriate form teacher, to be handed out in the afternoon, or sent back to the English teacher, so the students can receive their certificates during the following English lesson. The students then take the certificate home, to show their parents.

Some departments count the number of certificates given to each student during the term. A student in each class will then receive a worthwhile reward. Sadly, most students will not think *The Complete Works of Charles Dickens* is a worthwhile reward. However, a CD of their choice will be seen as a valued prize.

Sanctions

Whole-class detentions rarely work because students perceive these detentions as unfair. They then resent the teacher who gave the detention, thus causing problems for that teacher – who has risked alienating the whole class, including well-behaved students. I managed to fall into this trap in my first 2 years of teaching. It is far better to punish only those individuals who misbehave!

Detentions should be used for students who misbehave in a lesson and after they have been given two warnings – unless the offence is serious, such as throwing a chair across the room or attacking another student. In those cases, a teacher needs to call for help from a senior teacher.

Short detentions are the most effective and should end with the teacher talking to the student, outlining the offence and making it crystal clear why the offence was unacceptable and deserved a detention.

A phone call to parents is generally useful, as it shows the misbehaving student and the parent that you, as a teacher, care about the student's behaviour and his/her future progress in English.

Serious sanctions, which form part of the school discipline procedure, are part of senior management policy. The sanctions vary a great deal from school to school. However, an English department can create its own ethos by the following – and I apologize for repetition, but I feel it is so important to establish an effective ethos:

- Setting work that is creative, interesting and at the right level for the age and ability of the student.
- Having an assessment policy in place that involves the student and is understood by the student.
- Focusing on a seating plan that will effectively reduce the scope for misbehaviour within the classroom.
- Encouraging students to produce work for display purposes, which shows off student work.
- Sharing lesson objectives with the students and reinforcing learning through plenary sessions.
- Setting up an effective and efficient homework routine.
- Using whiteboard technology.
- Making all students aware of teacher expectations and rules.
- Making all students aware of rewards and punishments, then sticking to the procedures.

Should a small number of students fail to respond, then you will need to call on the head of English as your first port of call. An effective English department is one where there is a sense of collective responsibility. The student concerned should be given an appropriate sanction. I gave English department detentions, where English department work was set. Then I made the student write an apology to the English teacher, I kept a copy on file. Finally, I made the student verbally apologize to the member of my department.

If any student still misbehaves then, after liaison with the appropriate head of year, parents should be contacted and a meeting should be arranged between the parent(s), head of English, head of year and the classroom teacher. The threat of this sort of action is often enough to halt bad behaviour.

Department reports are another effective way of solving any misbehaviour. At the end of each English lesson, the student has to take a signed card to the head of English. Should the head of English not approve of the mark gained by the student, then the student is asked to undertake a short detention at a time convenient to the head of English. If the report is 'forgotten' or 'lost' then the student receives a short detention.

Another solution, for any student who persistently misbehaves, is to take that student from the English class and place him/her with the head of English. If the head of English is teaching at that particular time, then the misbehaving student will be placed at a convenient position in the classroom. Let us imagine the student is a misbehaving Year 9 boy. Should the head of English be teaching a Year 7 class, the Year 9 boy will go into the Year 7 class and he will be placed next to a Year 7 girl. Or if the head of English is teaching Year 13, the boy will go to the back of that class. He will be given work that he can do alone and without any interruptions. Away from his peer group he will be quiet. After the lesson he will be told that this arrangement can carry on all term if necessary. Generally, the misbehaviour ceases at one sitting!

Some English departments are able to deal with discipline by sharing out any problems. For example, if that Year 9 boy misbehaves and the head of English is free but needs to meet a parent, then the second in department would take the boy, or a teacher with experience and a track record for good discipline would step in. Students soon realize that there is no messing this department around!

The vast majority of misbehaviour ends if these procedures are carried out. The problem is also contained and dealt with within the department.

CHAPTER 4

Making it all seem like fun

Sentences

I really do believe that many students grasp concepts through drama-related activities. This is especially true for those with learning difficulties. Before introducing or reinforcing sentences, try some sentence games. Below are some games you can use.

Literal chairs

Place chairs in a circle. Choose one person to stand in the middle. If you know the group, choose somebody confident but compliant. The rest of the group will need to sit on their chairs. Take the spare chair away. The student in the middle calls: 'I like . . .' A second student (selected with raised hand, to avoid students shouting out) will complete the sentence. An example could be: 'I like Chinese takeaways.' Tell students that they have formed a sentence. It is a sentence because it makes sense.

To make the game fun, ask students to raise their hands if they like Chinese takeaways. Students who like Chinese takeaways need to change places with other students who like Chinese takeaways. There is just one rule for this game, a student cannot change places with the student sitting next to him/her.

The caller now needs to quickly find a seat. The student without a seat becomes the next caller.

Once students get into the game, they should produce some interesting examples. These might be:

I like owning a pet dog.

I like watching exciting films.

I like surfing on the beach.

Reinforce all the time that they are making sentences. You may like to type the sentences onto a whiteboard, so they can see the sentences written down.

The above game can be used with mixed-ability Year 7 students or with lower-ability students, from Year 7–Year 9.

The like/dislike game

Another game to reinforce sentences is a well known game, called 'Like/dislike'.

Keeping students sitting in the circle, the caller starts a sentence and another student completes it. The caller could say, 'I like Manchester United'. You then pick a student who has a hand raised. The second student could then say, 'But dislike Arsenal'. The complete sentence would be, 'I like Manchester United but dislike Arsenal.'

You could have sentences as in the following:

I like eating chocolate but dislike eating cabbage.

I like English lessons but dislike maths lessons.

If students are able to grasp these ideas you can make them more varied. Use the 'like' but do away with the dislike.

I like holidays and spend them swimming in the water.

I like making money and enjoy spending it.

Once students have understood sentences, you can move on to capital letters and full stops. The 'Sit up/sit down' game can be useful as a warm up. This game will help students understand that capital letters are used at the start of a sentence and full stops are mostly used at the end of each sentence.

In this game, students jump up at the start of a sentence and sit down at the end of a sentence, where there should be a full stop.

Here are some sentences you could use for this game. They are available online in case you would like to display the sentences on the board.

I'm good at spotting capital letters.

A tiger prowled around the zoo.

You go to town every evening.

I saw a fight in the playground.

The car was out of control.

If members of the group are ready for question marks and exclamation marks, they can tap their heads for a question mark and touch their ears for an exclamation mark. The exercise might generate some noise, but it will be an effective way of learning.

Following are some sentences you could use. These are also available online.

- Do you go out every night?
- You, come here!
- Do as I say! At once!
- Did you see the robbery yesterday?

To help weaker students, try to use the tone of voice someone would use for each of the above sentences.

When it comes to writing sentences, you can make the lesson fun by choosing sentences that would appeal to them in some way.

While working with students with learning difficulties, ask them to pick out a sentence from the examples below, which are also available online:

- Mrs Grease a café.
- Lord Slipperyfeet into a slimy ditch.
- Jeremy Wolf howls at the moon.
- The striker fell over bootlace.

Ask them which sentence makes sense and why. Point out that in each of the other three examples, *one* word can make the group of words become complete sentences, as shown below:

- Mrs Grease **owns** a café.
- Lord Slipperyfeet **fell** into a slimy ditch.
- The striker fell over **his** bootlace.

There are further complete sentence examples online.

Students can then write out the following sentences, putting in one word, so that each sentence makes sense:

- Belinda Blabbermouth tells everyone about.
- The dragon the village.
- Miss Oldperson's clothes of mothballs.
- My horse is Winraces.

To reinforce the use of capital letters, following are sentences students can read through and put in the capital letters, which are also available online. They can imagine that a famous author was in a hurry. The writer has made some mistakes as she had to write quickly in order to meet a deadline.

> stephen felt a hand on his shoulder. he knew he was in trouble.
> he heard the click of a gun. there was no way out of this mess.
> nothing could save him now.

Allow the students to point out where the capital letters need to go. Then try them on the sentences below. These sentences are available online, in case you would like to display them on the whiteboard:

- mrs toplady's head was bald.
- jake lost money in las vegas.
- sandra felt sick because she ate too many easter eggs.
- it is fun to roam around new zealand.
- the wrestling champion from birmingham is called luke noholds.

There are further capital letters examples online.

Once again, students can imagine that a famous writer was in a hurry. This time, she forgot to use full stops.

The gunman fired Stephen fell to the ground The gunman fled from the room Stephen stood up He felt dizzy but he was alive The bullet-proof vest had saved him

Point out that, as in the games they have played, question marks and exclamation marks are sometimes used instead of full stops. Tell the students that most of their sentences will end in full stops. If they use a one-word sentence or a command, they will generally need to use an exclamation mark. If they ask a question, they will need a question mark. All other sentences need full stops to end them.

You might wish to use the following sentences to reinforce what they have learned, which are also available online.

- Will it rain this afternoon
- Come here
- Yesterday it snowed heavily
- Get inside this house
- Did you hear about poor Annie

There are further question mark and exclamation sentences online.

Interesting sentences

For more able students you might wish to focus on stories that start in an interesting way. Point out that many stories start with a person's name or with he, she or it. If these starts can be avoided, they will gain the reader's attention.

Ask students to look at the starts to four different stories. Find four that you feel open in an interesting way. Focus on the sentences and ask students which sentences are interesting. Ask them which one they liked best and why. Hopefully, they won't all choose the same one – and a debate will ensue.

Paragraphs

The suggestions for paragraphing will be useful for Year 7 students.

Before launching into paragraphing, do not assume that students know what paragraphs are. They have amazingly short memories when it comes to remembering how to use paragraphs. You need to define them or allow students to find out for themselves from a range of definitions on a projector. Tell them that a paragraph is a group of sentences about one main idea or subject. Remind them that writers use paragraphs to signal to readers when they are going to write about another idea or subject. For instance, writers are likely to start a new paragraph when they begin to describe a new incident in a story.

Now give them an example. You could give them an exciting, interesting or mad paragraph that will grab their attention – as in the example below. This is provided online in case you would like to display it on the board or print it out for the students.

> Welcome to my world. On my planet we eat hedgehogs, bats and pigeons as our main diet. We cook hedgehogs in clay, we roast bats and we fry pigeon breasts. We eat them with vegetables from our farms. We throw the leftovers to our ever hungry, hunting dogs.

You will need to explain to the students that the most important sentence is the topic sentence. Ask them to pick out the topic sentence in the above paragraph. It is the main subject of the paragraph. They should work out that it is the second sentence. Point out that the other sentences are called supporting sentences as they tell you more about the topic. The final sentence is called the ending sentence.

Allow students to write four or five sentences about another alien world, a world in which they train minibeasts to perform in their circuses. Ask students to underline the topic sentence of their paragraph.

Your class should reinforce what they have learned by underlining supporting sentences. Do try the example below, which is also available online.

> Jake wandered into a large forest. The forest was dark and Jake became afraid. He imagined he saw shapes behind the trees and shapes crawling along the ground. He heard a snarling noise. He smelled the hot breath of a wild animal. He was sorry he'd ventured into the forest alone.

They should underline all the sentences except the first (topic sentence) and last (ending sentence).

Now allow students to write their own paragraph about somebody who is afraid. After they have written their paragraph, ask students to swap books with a partner. The partner will need to highlight the different types of sentences using different coloured pens. They will need three different coloured pens for this activity. To avoid confusion, they could use a blue pen for the topic sentence, a green pen for the supporting sentences and a red pen for the ending sentence. Or students could use the highlighter function on the whiteboard (or palette) to pick out the different sentences and use different colours for the various types of sentences.

In a fun way, students should have mastered the different sentences used to make up a paragraph. I know, whenever I have used this activity, students have enjoyed the work and learned how to write using paragraphs.

Further work to reinforce the use of paragraphs can be achieved through mime.

In pairs, students can mime a situation where one of them has seen an older student steal a wad of notes from a teacher's desk. The older student has noticed that he has been observed stealing the notes. What does he do? What happens next? Will he want to share the money? Will he appear to threaten the younger student or will he run away?

Students may need reminding that in mime it is actions that count. No words are spoken.

When the mimes are over, ask students to write down all that happened in the mime. They will need a topic sentence, supporting sentences and an ending sentence.

Allow them to write more that one paragraph if they wish.

To help students order their paragraphs, divide a story into four paragraphs and then jumble the paragraphs. Allow students to work in pairs and ask them to see if they can place the paragraphs in their correct order. Students will work out that paragraphs in most stories are linked. This exercise should help them to think about linking their own paragraphs into a logical order.

If you would like to try this with students, use the example below. This is also available online in case you would like to display it on the whiteboard or print it out and give to the students as a handout.

The stalker

a. When he stopped, the movement behind him stopped. Josh was painfully aware that he was alone. Alone, walking down a narrow lane. He stooped to pick up a large stick. He was determined to defend himself to the bitter end.

b. Mrs Clarkson kept Josh behind because he hadn't completed his English homework. He felt resentful. He hated the pirate project and hadn't wanted to write anything. But he wrote quickly when he knew Mrs Clarkson wouldn't let him go until the work was complete. As soon as he'd finished writing, Josh threw his book on the teacher's desk and stormed out of school. He was late and his mates hadn't waited for him.

c. A voice called his name. The call was soft and urgent. Josh turned to face his dad. Josh still recognized his dad, even after all these years. Dad had been in some kind of trouble, he'd run away. Now he was back. Josh dropped his stick, his weapon, and stared into his dad's pale blue eyes. What was his dad doing here? What did dad want from him? All these thoughts flashed through Josh's mind as he stared at his dad.

d. Josh was still in a bad mood when he walked through the main street and entered the gloomy lane that cut into the playing fields. He was in such a temper that he hadn't noticed the soft pad, pad of feet behind him. The moment he did notice, he was scared.

The students should quickly spot the paragraph order – b, d, a and c.

For a similar exercise, there is another task online.

Roll of the dice
If you ask students to write the start of a story, talk about how many paragraphs they should write. To make the process more exciting, bring in a couple of dice. Ask each student to roll the dice. Tell them they have to throw again if the dice falls on one or two. A roll above that figure is the number of paragraphs that person will need to write. All students will need to write between three and six paragraphs! Surprisingly, the students accept the number they have rolled. This is because, by rolling the dice, they have determined (by random chance) the number of paragraphs they need to write – you haven't!

Recognizing an interesting story start
Recognizing and then writing their own interesting start to a story is useful for writing development, especially at KS3. How is this done? By keeping students interested. By allowing students to debate which story they like best and then voting on which they believe is the best story is a way forward. Try the example below!

Allow students to look at the following story openings. Which do they believe works best? These are all available online.

a. *The Secret* by Myles Burbage
    Another bullet hit the shack and penetrated into the woodwork. Jasmine knew she had to do something quickly, or she would die. The assassins were closing in. She looked at the golden key clenched

into her hand. If she didn't give them the key, they would kill her. If she gave them the key, they would kill her anyway. Only she knew the secret, so she had to die.

b. *Sea Saw* by Jenny Protherough

The sea was rough and diving was dangerous. Geoff Millist lived for danger. He knew danger, he smelt danger, he got high on danger. He'd diced with death many times. He needed to find the wreck and its treasures before the others did. This was his chance to get rich.

c. *A Retreat* by Tasmin Lane

The climb is tough. Each finger hold on the rock face is precarious. One step in the wrong place means certain death.

Yet, at the top of the rock stands the old monastery. A retreat for the monks who'd worshipped there for centuries. Or, at least, that's the story put out for tourists. There is a story, though – if journalists want to find one. It's much more sinister than the locals will ever tell you. Climb to the retreat and find the truth – if you dare!

d. *The Ring* by Jamie Longster

Too many deaths, too many! The old man studied the ring, shining in his shaking hands. Made of pure gold, but cursed. Sneaked out of Eastern Europe when the Berlin Wall fell and bought to England in the mid 1990s. Since then? Greed took over!

Ask students which start they liked best. They can either debate in small groups or in pairs. During the debate, ask students which story they would like to read.

On a basic level, which genre do the books belong to? Obviously not comedy. Are they all adventure books, or are some murder mysteries or horror? There is no right or wrong answer. There is no right book to select as the best start. The object of the exercise is to get students to think about how a good start works, which will improve their own writing. The intention of any writer is to sell his/her book. He/she will want the fiction book to be so exciting or interesting that you won't want to put the book down. Students should pick the story opening that they think will develop into such an exciting book that they will want to read it from cover to cover.

To make the lesson memorable and interesting, students can then vote for the 'Awesome Start Award'. Voting by secret ballot, students can then vote and decide which author gets the award.

Once the winning author has been selected, students can imagine they are writing an invitation to the winning author, inviting him/her to the award ceremony.

Writing the letter should take up part of a lesson, or be used as a homework. If you need to model this exercise for the students, try the example below. This is also available online in case you would like to display it on the board or print it out for the students.

Dear Tasmin,

Our class thought your story had an awesome start and we would like you to attend our 'Awesome Start Award'.

We felt that the first two sentences were exciting because whoever was climbing the rock face was dicing with death.

'Each finger hold on the rock face is precarious.'

Then there is the surprise that at the top of the rock stands a monastery. Or does there?

'That's the story put out for tourists.'

We do not know what the secret is but we do know it is not good.

'More sinister than the locals will ever tell you.'

Finally, a challenge is offered and we suspect that the unnamed person climbing the rock face wishes to discover what is happening. Our class has not read any other book that starts in such an exciting way.

Please do let us know if you can attend our meeting to receive the Awesome Start Award. The venue is Millhouse Comprehensive School, Haverfield. It takes place on 20 June 2010 at 6.30pm. Light refreshments will be served after the award.

Yours sincerely,

Class 9A

RSVP

A follow-up lesson could begin by students being reminded that it is important to start a story in an exciting way, to grab the reader's attention. One or two students could read out their letters, inviting the author to the award ceremony. Then, in pairs, one could take the role of the author and the other the award judge. They can act out the presentation ceremony. The 'author' could make an impromptu speech and collect an award. The award could be a small prize you can hand out to the class, or a pretend award. Roles are then reversed.

To help students with the idea of a developing plot, it is a good idea to ask them to select one of the stories and bullet point how they think the story will develop to keep the 'middle' interesting. Following are some possible ideas:

- The climber and hero, Alex Duncarde, arrives at the top of the mountain.
- The old monastery is deserted. There are human skeletons on the floor.
- Alex is about to leave the monastery but his path is blocked by three aliens.

Allow the students to re-read the story openings and then set them the task of writing a story opening about two people in a light aircraft that is being shot at, has been hit and is spinning out of control. They need to bullet point about five or six ideas and then write the story. Remind them, this is a story opening and not the whole plot!

Now ask the students to look at two versions of *The Secret*. This should be the amazing middle, but which middle is far from amazing? Which one has the yawn factor?

First of all, some facts that the students will need to know as the story progresses. These are also available online.

- Jasmine was rescued from the gunmen by a recluse called Dan Stammers.
- Stammers has allowed her to stay in his hut. However, he won't let her leave.
- Jasmine realizes she is a prisoner and Dan never seems to sleep.

a. The fire was nothing now. The wood was almost burned through. Just hot ashes. Jasmine glanced at the shovel on the hearth. Not too far, not out of her reach. Jasmine looked at Dan. He was looking at the ring on her finger.

   'Can't let you leave,' he said.

   'Why not?' asked Jasmine.

   'The ring, I know all about the ring,' said Dan. 'It's worth a lot of money, I could buy a big house.'

   Jasmine sighed. 'The ring might buy you a big house, but it's cursed. It'll bring you death.'

   Dan laughed but his laughter dried up quickly. Jasmine had the shovel in her hand. She's scooped up the hot ashes and flung them into Dan's plain face.

   Dan screamed as Jasmine made for the door.

b. The once-raging fire was nothing now. Just hot ashes. Jasmine glanced at the small, black shovel. Not too far, not out of her reach. Jasmine glared at Dan. He was looking straight at her long, delicate index finger. The finger that wore the golden ring. He knew!

   'Can't let you leave,' he said roughly, looking down at his big black boots.

'Why not?' asked Jasmine, faking surprise and running her long fingers through her wispy auburn hair.

'The ring, I know all about the ring,' hissed Dan. 'It's worth a load of dosh. It could buy me a huge house in the country.'

Jasmine sighed. She knew Dan was an enemy but he'd saved her from certain death. She almost felt sorry for the big man.

'The ring might buy you a mansion in the country, but it's cursed. It'll bring you death.'

Dan laughed but his laughter dried up as quickly as dew on a hot day. Jasmine had the black shovel in her hand. She scooped up the red hot ashes from the fire and flung them into Dan's moon-like face.

Dan screamed like a demon as his podgy hands clutched at his hurting face. Jasmine ran for the old wooden door.

Hopefully, the students will appreciate that b is more detailed and, therefore, more interesting than a.

- The first example tells us the same story but the second one makes the story more exciting. It does this by giving us more detail.
- The use of adjectives and similes adds to our mind's eye picture of the events as they unfold.
- The choice of words tells us something of the thoughts and description of both Jasmine and Dan.

Ask the students to write an interesting middle to their story, using similes and adjectives, and thinking about word choice. It is worth pointing out that the second example is **almost** over the top. Too many adjectives can make a piece of writing jar!

They should then think about an end that has impact.

Get the students to thought-shower what could happen next in the story to make a memorable end. They could use a spider diagram to help them remember their thought-shower.

Following are some ideas:

- Having escaped from Dan, Jasmine hides the ring in a hole in a tree not far from Dan's hut.
- Jasmine is captured by Orwell Sparkes, the man behind the gang who tried to kill her in the shack. He forces her into the boot of his car and drives her to his house.
- Jasmine escapes and manages to text her friend, Damien Wells, before being recaptured.
- Orwell Sparks tries to threaten Jasmine and manages to half-drown her before the police and Damien arrive and rescue her.

- The ring is given back to a German business man, who presents Jasmine with a large reward. Dan tries to steal the reward but is arrested.

Allow the students to read the ending and ask them to thought-shower a better ending than the original!

Ask the students to bullet point about five ideas to complete their own story and then ask them to swap stories with a partner and challenge the partner to write a better ending to their own story than the one they have written.

As an incentive, allow the students to redraft their stories using their ICT skills and then display the stories. Students can use Word to type and redraft their stories. The final product can become part of a classroom display. Students can see their work held in high esteem (putting their work on display indicates to students that their work is worth something). They can then read their fellow students' work, which will enable them to appreciate why their work has gained a particular mark. In one sense, a display can be a modelling exercise. Students then know what they need to do to achieve a higher mark next time.

A spelling game

Students need to know which letters are vowels. They are: a, e, i, o and u. Vowels may be sounded long as in fate or short as in fat. You can change a long vowel to a short one by taking away the final e.

Long vowel sounds are in bide, bite, cute, dote, fate, hate, kite, mate, note, pate and rate.

Short vowel sounds are in bid, bit, cut, dot, fat, hat, kit, mat, not, pat and rat.

As a drama exercise, to reinforce this spelling lesson, divide the class into two. Half the class are to hold up a card with the letter 'e' and the other half has words with short vowel sounds. The 'e' half of the class need to find someone with a small vowel sound, in order to make a new word. They can do this several times, until they get the idea of long/short vowel sounds.

As a variation of this exercise, put in some words with short vowel sounds that cannot be matched and allow students to discover for themselves that some words cannot be changed by adding an 'e'. For example, red and fed cannot be changed.

The above exercise does need some preparation but it is rewarding.

As a written exercise, you can follow this up by asking students to put in the missing letters to the following piece of writing, which is also available online.

My mat— flew a kit—, got hungry and went for a bit— . He said he'd hat— to dot— on his sister's cut— baby.

There might be good, average and poor spellers in a class. An old-fashioned spelling test is not usually a good idea. A better idea is to tackle individual spelling needs. Students should be aware of the 'look-think-say-cover-write-check' method. However, do not take for granted that they are aware of this!

If possible, give each student a spelling book. When mistakes are spotted, get the students to write the correct spelling in their books.

Allow the students to follow this method. Tell them to:

- Look at the correct spelling of the word with care.
- Think about any part of the word that might have caused a problem.
- Say the word out loud or in your head.
- Check how you went wrong.
- Now cover the word up.
- Write the word out without looking at it.
- Check to see if you have got it right.
- If you have still got the spelling wrong, go through the method again.

You might need to state the obvious – if they cheat, they cheat themselves. The object of the exercise is to improve their spelling in the long term.

When an individual student has mastered the spellings, tell him/her to check that he/she can still spell the words in a week's time and then in a month's time. The correct spelling needs to lodge itself in the student's long-term memory.

Hangman

It is worth playing spelling games such as 'Hangman'. This game can be played on the blackboard or the whiteboard. Make sure that students select a word and place the number of dashes that match with the number of letters in the chosen word. For example, a five-letter word should have five dashes on the board. The group needs to give you a letter, one at a time.

Tell the class that it is better to use vowels in the first few guesses. A correctly guessed letter should go above the dash. A letter that does not make up the word should be recorded and the hangman's gibbet begins!

You can cut down the possibilities by asking students to select a famous footballer, pop star or pop group. Check that each word chosen is correctly spelled by asking the selected student to write it down and slip you the piece of paper.

This game is essentially a spelling game and it allows students to focus on how to spell a word if they are to avoid the hangman's noose.

The game works well with Year 7 and with lower-ability students.

Word finding game

Split the class into two. Each of one half holds up a card with est printed on it. Each of the other half has one or two letters on a card. They all have to find a partner to complete a word.

Examples:
   Ch-est = Chest; Bl-est = Blest;
   Cr-est = Crest; Gu-est = Guest;
   J-est = Jest; V-est = Vest.

You can also do the same exercise using 'ock' and 'ap'.

Examples:
   Cl-ock = Clock; Fl-ock = Flock;
   Cl-ap = Clap; Tr-ap = Trap.

You can add variety to the game by turning singular words into plurals. Again, half the class can hold up cards with singular words, the other half can have either 's' or 'es' written on their cards.

Examples:
   Apple = Apples; Toe = Toes;
   Eye = Eyes; Fox = Foxes.

A spin-off value for this game could be that students gain a better understanding of the apostrophe s. They may realize that the apostrophe s is not used for plurals!

Boy-friendly poems

If you mention that you are going to look at poems, you will probably receive a collective groan from the boys in your class. But if you choose the right poems you will get a different response. Anything to do with nature, and especially flowers, just won't grab them.

I still like the book *Axed Between the Ears* (Kitchen, 1987), which features some poems boys really enjoy. There is a book of football poems called *Ere We Go* chosen by David Orme (1993). Another book I have used is *The Spot on My Bum* by Gez Walsh (1997). The title alone silences the groans. Finally, *Hot Heads Warm Hearts Cold Streets* edited by John Foster (1996) has poems that really work for older students. 'Let No One Steal Your Dreams', a poem by Paul Cookson (1996), works with Years 10 and 11 groups.

There are many rap poems published these days. Raps usually work with boys and most groups enjoy writing their own raps. You should be able to find some good examples online.

Ballad or narrative poems usually work well, as they deal with action or events. Avoid the love ballads as a general rule.

Following is an interesting traditional ballad that I have used many times. It is quite short and some good work can come from it. It is also available online.

The Mermaid

Twas Friday morn when we set sail,
And we had not gone far from land,
When the Captain, he spied a lovely mermaid,
With a comb and a glass in her hand.

Then up spoke the Captain of our gallant ship,
And a jolly old Captain was he;
'I have a wife in Salem town,
But tonight a widow she will be.'

Then up spoke the Cook of our gallant ship,
And a greasy old cook was he;
'I care more for my kettles and my pots,
Than I do for the roaring of the sea.'

Then up spoke the Cabin-boy of our gallant ship,
And a dirty little brat was he:
'I have friends in Boston Town
That don't care a ha'penny for me.'

Then three times 'round went our gallant ship.
And three times round went she,
And the third time that she went 'round
She sank to the bottom of the sea.

Author unknown

Point out to students that titles are usually important. Has the ship been cursed because the sailors and the captain have seen a mermaid? Otherwise, why the title?

They can note that every second and fourth line rhymes. Every stanza is four lines long. It is set out like a song and was sung as a folk song.

Can the storyline be worked out? It might be that the ship is travelling from England to America. The Captain has a wife in Salem and the Cabin-boy has 'friends' in Boston.

Is the narrator a ghost or did he survive the sinking?

As an introduction to poetry, it can be contrasted with a modern disaster. There may be an aeroplane crash in the news or a shipping tragedy. If not, find a newspaper cutting of the Zeebrugge disaster or information on the sinking of the *Titanic*.

You can get a variety of work from this poem, which could include:

- A newspaper article of the sinking of the ship.
- A survivor's story.
- A rap of the event.

Longer poems can be broken up into shorter sections. If you take part one of the poem, *The Rime of the Ancient Mariner*, by Samuel Taylor Coleridge (1798), you can ask the students to form small groups of four and take a stanza each. Ask them to read their stanza and then act out what they think is happening. Give them a time limit of 15 minutes to work on their drama presentation. Then bring them back together as a class and read part one of the poem to them. Finally, ask them to act out their stanzas sequentially. They will soon work out what the poem is about!

Group A will act out the first 'scene', having worked out that an old sailor has stopped a wedding guest from attending a wedding. The guest has noticed that the old sailor has a 'long beard and a glittering eye'.

At any time, you can ask the group to freeze-frame a particular moment and you can ask questions.

Example:
Q: How does the wedding guest feel?
A: He's uncomfortable. He wants to be with the other guests. He might be afraid of the old sailor.

Students might point out that in the second stanza the wedding guest is urging the old sailor to let him go. He ought to be at the wedding because he is next of kin.

The actors involved in the third stanza should enjoy themselves.

Hold off! Unhand me, grey-beard loon!

Ask the students what they think that particular line means. Most students would say that 'hold off' means 'let go'. And 'grey-beard loon' means grey-bearded madman or lunatic.

By now the students will be fully engaged with the poem. The fourth team of actors will notice that the wedding guest is hypnotized.

He holds him with his glittering eye.

The wedding guest is forced to listen to the story.

The mariner has his will.

Students will feel that the mariner holding a wedding guest against his will is an exciting start to a poem. All this before the main story begins!

The students will quickly work out that the mariner's ship was in a dangerous position. It was surrounded by ice in an unknown region of the world. (At this point, I sometimes read them an account of the Ernest Shackleton true story, the part when the ship is breaking up in the ice.) When the albatross arrives, the sailors see it as a good luck omen.

Most of the students will turn against the mariner when they read that he has shot the albatross. As with any good story, they will want to carry on. They will want to know what happens.

The poem has all the ingredients for success – deaths, the supernatural, ghosts, a strange spell and demons. In addition, there are strange sea-creatures and the fact that the ship and its crew are stranded mid-ocean.

The ancient mariner has to pay a price for killing the albatross. He has to tell people his story and warn them to love 'All things both great and small'. He cannot die, which means it could be *you* that he speaks to next week!

I have usually asked groups to act out sections of the poems, so that they can grasp the storyline. When the storyline is understood, then I'll give them time to look at the poetry technique.

There is a variety of work that could come from this poem. Work could include:

- Write a description of the land of fearful sounds, where no living thing is to be seen.
- Imagine you are the wedding guest; describe events from your point of view.
- Take one part of the poem and rewrite it either as a modern story or as a rap.
- You are a newspaper reporter; interview the ancient mariner about the events and all that happens aboard ship.
- You are making a film of *The Rime of the Ancient Mariner*. Storyboard the film and then list the actors you would like to see in the film.

Example: Ancient Mariner = Johnny Depp.

Stimulus

With younger students (Years 7 and 8) a stimulus is sometimes needed to get them started on a poem. You cannot assume that they are all bursting to write, using their imagination. Some are obviously imaginative but many, sadly, are not!

A picture stimulus often works, providing it is of a dramatic event – such as a dragon about to devour a young girl, with a knight in the distance. The knight looks worried and the picture suggests he might not arrive in time. The dragon's mouth drips blood.

A Constable painting of the countryside, good as it is, is very unlikely to inspire boys. A fantasy picture probably will!

Another way to get boys into poetry is the stimulus of a poetry bag. This really means a list of interesting words that students can then use to make a poem. If you cut up the words, put them in a bag and spill the words onto their desks: it works much better than putting the heading 'Poetry bag' on the whiteboard and placing the words underneath the title. The students appear to react well to the seemingly random nature of the poetry bag. If they work in pairs, you will need a number of poetry bags with the same choice of words in the bags – but that does not appear to matter to the students.

Of course, students do not need to use all the words, and they can add new words that they have thought up.

Following is a list of words that have worked for me:

Ice Creature Sea Wet Cold Rock
Swishing Dull Sand Splashing Waves Windy
Monster Cried Cry Seagull

Following are two responses from two Year 7 students.

Lone Island
An *icy* grip,
Held in the *wet* land,
A *seagull cried.*

Splashing waves
Covered the green *rock*.

A *sea creature* rose,
Rose from
The *cold wet sea.*

By Ian Blackburn (Year 7)

Monster Island
I watched the *seagull cry,*
I watched the *swishing* waves.
I watched the *monster* rise,
The *creature* from the *sea.*

By Alison Cattermole (Year 7)

The more words you can say spilled from the poetry bag, the more likely you are to have a variety of interesting poems returned to you. Treat the poems as precious and, if possible, use them as part of a classroom display. Do not be afraid to allow students to illustrate their poems.

As a variation on the theme, tell students that the word bag has split open. The word bag was very full and many words have spilled out.

Here they are:

Wild Stark Hopeless Beast Moor Old
Untamed Landscape Grimy Blessing Track Feeding
Clumsy Footprints Cubs Imitate Fern Skull Bones Dry Bower
Harsh Growl Hiss Lair Followed

Ask the students to look at these words carefully and write a poem using some of them. The words are also available online in case you would like to display them on the board. Before they begin writing, ask them the following questions:

- What do these words suggest to you?
- What type of poem might come from these words?
- Can you add your own words to make an interesting poem?

If any students are stuck, give them a title such as 'The creature of Brickly Moor'.

Following is an example of a poem written by a Year 8 student.

The Beast
Wild and *untamed*,
The fanged *beast*
Rose from its *lair*.

The *beast's cubs*
Followed, afraid.

Their footsteps trod
The harsh *landscape*.
They scuttled behind
Their *beast* mum.

She was looking for food,
*Track*ing, smelling, waiting.

The cubs *imitat*ing.

By Jonnie Bostock (Year 8)

With weaker groups, list poems are a good way to get students started.

Tell them that they are going to make a list of things that they like and dislike. They can then build a poem. Give the students a sheet of paper. Ask them to write down two headings – 'Likes' and 'Dislikes'. The students can then thought-shower for about 10 minutes, noting down all the likes and dislikes that come into their heads. They should be encouraged to write down *all* their ideas. Students then need to spend a further 5 minutes editing and ordering their lists. They may not use all that they have written down. For example, they may decide to go for a theme – likes/dislikes about school or sport or where they live. They may need to take things out or think of new ideas. Encourage them to do this and give them time to change their minds!

When the poems are complete, students should be encouraged to share their poems with a partner. The partner may suggest some changes. Finally, poems can be redrafted using students' IT skills.

Following are examples from two Year 7 students. Please model these to the students, as examples of list poems. Challenge them to do better, after all the examples are from their own age group.

Likes and Dislikes
I like peas but hate cabbage,
I love milk but loathe tea.
I adore ice cream but can't stand blancmange.
I eat curries but spit out chops,
I like bacon but loathe egg.

By Stuart Fellingham (Year 7)

Likes and Dislikes
I like stroking my pet cat,
I like hot sunny days.
I like swimming in the river,
I like playing fast football.
I like riding my bike,
I like fun times with my mates.

I dislike moaning minnies,
I dislike dirty towns.
I dislike violent wars,
I dislike seeing people unhappy.
I dislike watching boring films,
I dislike mean people.

By Adojan Szabo (Year 7)

Shape poems are fun to do with Years 7 and 8 students. They enjoy working out the shapes. However, for brighter students there ought to be a meaning with the shape and a creativity in order to produce a good shape poem.

Following are two examples:

Firework

```
                                    g
        S                 S         u        b                    r
     b    p               h         n        r                    a
     u      a             o         p      e     w                i
      r   r               w         o      e     h                n
  f   s   k               e         w    z     i                  b
  l   t                   r         d    e     z                  o
   y   s   f                        e    d     z                  w
    i    t    l          b          r    r     b                  c
    n     a    a         l          s    i     a                  r
     g     r    m       o           p      f     n                a
      s        i      s            a       t       g              c
      p           n    s           r       e                      k
       a          g  o             k       r                      l
        r            m             l                              e
         k                   e
          l
           e


              s p l u t t e r
                                      dead
```

By Ruth West (2010a)

Water

```
        e r y           a s h      a n d
      t     w      w       i n g      s
    a        a v e s                 p
  w                              l a s h
                                       i
                                         n
                                           g
```

Water that sloshes and sloshes and spots
Clouds that get blacker and BLACKER and BLACKER
Thunder that CLAPS!
Rain that pours

Rain that pours

```
            d
              o
                w
                  n
                    a
                      n
                        d
                          d
                            o
                              w
                                n
                                  a
                                    n
                                      d
                                        d
                                          o
                                            w
                                              n
```

By Ruth West (2010b)

Now ask the students to think about a shape poem of their own. They may well enjoy drawing their own shape and then forming the poem around the shape, or they may like to think of a theme and then create the shape to fit in with the theme.

Shape poems make great classroom displays. When students see their own poems as part of a classroom display, they are usually encouraged.

Poems using compound words make a good lesson. Try the following – it is useful for a lesson on how poetry breaks the rules. The compound words are used for effect.

Explain that Sean Casey gives us a vivid picture of Rocky the dog, in his poem 'Rocky, My Dog'. He does this by combining two or more words together. These are called compound words – and they are usually joined by a hyphen. *Example:* barking-dog.

Allow students to read the poem and then ask them to list all the compound words they can find in the poem. Ask them to think of another animal for a poem using compound words. They might think of a cat or a horse. Before writing a poem, they should think of their own compound words: words that will fit into their poem.

They may like to thought-shower words for a cat, such as:

Soft Whiskers Fur
Paws Milk Feline

Having done that, they can turn these single words into compound words.

This exercise works well with Year 7 students.

Rocky, My Dog
Rocky is the barking-dog,
The larking-around dog.
The tickly-my-tummy,
The stroke-me-please,
The jumper-over-ditches,
The scratcher of fleas dog.

Rocky with-a-bone
Is a snarling dog.
A keep-away-please,
A might-bite-you dog.

But when he's ill
And at the vets,
I want him back,
My play-around pet.

By Sean Casey

Able Year 9 students will need more of a challenge. Read the following poem to them.

Empty House

Inside the empty house,
Silence hung around like faded wallpaper
And gossamer-thin cobwebs.
Nothing except floorboards,
And yellow stains.

And yet the whispers
From gaps in the windows
And a fading reflection
In the long-dim hall,
Where a light fitting hung
Dangerous and decayed.

And the smell of the past.
Times gone and people,
Filter through my mind
Like phantom dwellers.

Children, kitchen-bound,
Hungry; mum bringing coal
To a lively fire. Dad
With his pipe smoke,
His dreams.

These touch my mind
With gravestone chill.

And I am afraid,
Inside the empty house.

By Sean Casey

Ask the students the following questions:

1. What is the poem about?
2. What senses does the poet appeal to in this poem?
   (Reminder: senses include your sight, hearing, smell and touch.)
3. Why do you think the memories touch the poet 'with gravestone chill'?
4. Why do you think the poet is afraid?

You might like the students to work in small groups or in pairs on the following two questions.

1. What ideas of the empty house is the poet trying to create in the second line? Why is the simile appropriate? (Remind students: a simile is a comparison using 'as' or 'like'. *Example:* 'as heavy as lead'. Or, 'he sank like a stone'.)
2. List the compound words used in the poem. Why is the use of these words effective?

You might like the students to work on their own to complete the following two activities. Tell them to:

1. Thought-shower a word bank of compound words to describe an eerie atmosphere. *Examples:* 'death-chill' and 'grave-cold'.
2. Decide on a theme for a ghostly poem and use your word bank of about ten compound words to help you write your poem.

As the poem is a mystery poem, you will find that able students will enjoy working on it.

A final exercise to engage boys with poetry is to cut up a poem and give them parts of it to put together again. When some poems are cut up, there is no right or wrong answer, but it promotes discussion if students are working in groups of four or in pairs.

Following is a poem that could be used in this exercise. It is a rhyming poem, so the students should be able to work it out although it is unlikely that many (if any) will have the poem back to the original! Their answers will be interesting.

The Mistletoe Bough
The mistletoe hung in the castle hall,
The holly branch shone on the old oak wall;
And the baron's retainers were blithe and gay,
And keeping their Christmas holiday.
The baron beheld with a father's pride
His beautiful child, young Lovell's bride;
While she with her bright eyes seem'd to be
The star of the goodly company.

'I'm weary of dancing now;' she cried;
'Here tarry a moment – I'll hide – I'll hide!
And, Lovell, be sure thou'rt first to trace
The clue to my secret lurking place.'
Away she ran – and her friends began
Each tower to search, and each nook to scan;
And young Lovell cried, 'Oh where dost thou hide?
I'm lonesome without thee, my own dear bride.'

They sought her that night! and they sought her next day!
And they sought her in vain when a week pass'd away!
In the highest – the lowest – the loneliest spot,
Young Lovell sought wildly – but found her not.
And years flew by, and their grief at last
Was told as a sorrowful tale long past;
And when Lovell appeared, the children cried,
'See! The old man weeps for his fairy bride.'

By Thomas Haynes Bayley

You will need to cut the poem up into two rhyming lines each and place them into bags. You will need about 15 bags! Then students will need to place the paper on their desks and reform the poem. Tell them they are poem detectives and they are piecing the poem back together like a jig-saw puzzle. An interesting discussion should take place as students work together to place the poem in the right place. You can tell them that you have given them three stanzas if you like.

When you cut the poem up, use the alphabet as in my example below. The poem is also available online.

A 'I'm weary of dancing now;' she cried;
'Here tarry a moment – I'll hide – I'll hide!

B While she with her bright eyes seem'd to be
The star of the goodly company.

C And when Lovell appeared, the children cried,
'See! the old man weeps for his fairy bride.'

D The mistletoe hung in the castle hall,
The holly branch shone on the old oak wall;

E Away she ran – and her friends began
Each tower to search, and each nook to scan;

F In the highest – the lowest – the loneliest spot,
Young Lovell sought wildly – but found her not.

G And, Lovell, be sure thou'rt first to trace
The clue to my secret lurking place.'

H And young Lovell cried, 'Oh where doest thou hide?
I'm lonesome without thee, my own dear bride.'

I And the baron's retainers were blithe and gay,
And keeping their Christmas holiday.

J They sought her that night! and they sought her next day!
And they sought her in vain when a week pass'd away!

K And years flew by, and their grief at last
Was told as a sorrowful tale long past;

L The baron beheld with a father's pride
His beautiful child, young Lovell's bride;

Students should find some clues in the punctuation.

With able groups, you can talk about the validity of their reconstruction versus the original poem.

More work can come from this. Ask the students what is happening in the poem. Then ask them to write an ending to it. When they have written their ending, show them the original:

At length an oak chest, that had long lain hid,
Was found in the castle – they raised the lid –
And a skeleton form lay mouldering there,
In the bridal wreath of that lady fair!
Oh! sad was her fate! –in sportive jest
She hid from her lord in the old oak chest.
It closed with a spring! – and, dreadful doom,
The bride lay clasp'd in her living tomb!

By Thomas Haynes Bayley

As an additional exercise, I have asked my students to write a modern version. The oak chest has become a large fridge-freezer!

With some groups, you may wish to choose a shorter modern poem than 'The Mistletoe Bough'. The rhymes give clues, so choose a rhyming poem for this exercise: perhaps a modern ballad by Charles Causley.

Making a drama out of verbs, nouns and adjectives

As a teacher, I quickly discovered that 'doing' exercises on verbs, nouns and adjectives did not necessarily translate into greater student understanding of these parts of speech. There are many exercises out there, in a variety of textbooks. Students can work through the books and get the exercises right. That does not always mean that they understand the use of verbs, nouns and adjectives, and that the work has gone into their long-term memory.

It is frustrating when you go through the parts of speech and assume that the work done and effort made will translate into a better piece of creative writing. Or that students will be able to recognize these parts of speech in an exam.

Of course, some students will do well and remember everything that has taken place in your classroom. However, if this is not the case you might like to try a different approach. I have done this, using drama as a learning tool.

Verbs – a mime exercise

A verb is a doing word, so let's do! Ask the students to mime the following:

Swimming – swim.

They can choose any style they like, such as the front crawl, the breast stroke or the back stroke.

Ask the students to mime playing a game. Then tell them to guess what each game is. You may get answers like the following examples:

'He *played* football.' Or 'She *played* a game on the computer.'

Tell the students the action is the verb – *swim* and *play*.

Nouns

Allow students to understand that there are five types of nouns. Today we are going to become a common noun. Give students a bag. They are going to play 'lucky dip'.

When the students look at the common noun they have picked out of the bag, they have to mime that common noun. The rest of the class will need to guess what the 'actor' has become.

The bag could contain words such as:

Cat Pen Man Dog Pencil Baby
Horse Desk Cottage Lady Soldier Computer

(You will need a different common noun for each student.)

When the exercise is complete, explain that common nouns can turn into proper nouns. The proper noun will have a specific name. For example, there are many breeds of cats but Marble is specific to one breed.

In groups, students can make up a short improvised play using the common nouns that they have just turned into proper nouns. For those who have picked common nouns that cannot become proper nouns (such as pen) then they might suggest their own proper noun.

Use mind association to help you remember words:

Cat = Marble; Man = Mr Sturmer; Dog = Growler; Cottage = Vine Cottage

Abstract nouns can also be used in the play, to suggest how the characters feel. Again, use mind association to help:

Anger = Growler; Bravery = Mr Sturmer; Fear = Marble

As an addition, a good lesson could be spent on telling students that a new planet has been discovered. It is near a sun and is very similar to Earth. It has oceans, rivers and plant life. The animals on this planet are very different from creatures on Earth. They need to be named. Name the animals and then describe them. Imagine you have made a pet of two of these animals. What would you call them?

The work on nouns should be viewed as a starter. I deal with nouns in much more detail in the section 'Bringing the Assessment Focus to Life'. I also revisit verbs and adjectives in this section.

Adjectives

Present students with a piece of text, as in the example below:

1. People stayed in their homes and warmed their hands by the fire. The snow swirled and the blizzard blew. Ridinghood wanted to visit her grandmother. She dressed in a coat with a hood. She grabbed a basket and walked into the wood.

   A wolf waited in the wood. He was hungry.

2. **Old** people stayed in their **cold** homes and warmed their **chapped** and **gnarled** hands by the **roaring** fire. The **ghost-white** snow swirled and the **fierce** blizzard blew. **Little Red Ridinghood** wanted to visit her **frail, sick** grandmother. She dressed in a **long, red** coat with a **pointed** hood. She grabbed a **fine new** basket and walked into the **still, white** wood.

   A **sly** wolf waited in the **wild** wood. He was hungry.

Explain to the students that they should not overdo the use of adjectives and that adjectives need to be used carefully. Adjectives can vastly improve their writing.

The above text is available online, should you wish to display it. There is also another online activity for work on adjectives.

Non-fiction materials that are boy friendly

Boys tend to enjoy real-life stories. They like reading about events that really happened. If you search the internet or a library, there are many true stories that can be turned into comprehension passages or used as stimulus for creative writing tasks. I have listed some ideas below.

Disasters

- The San Francisco earthquake. Seven hundred people died and most of the city was destroyed. The greatest damage came from fires that raged for 3 days.
- Disaster in Canada. Jack Hornby and his team of young explorers died in the Canadian wilderness (1927). One of the team kept a diary.
- The R101 air disaster, 1930. The airship was built to take passengers across the Atlantic to America. Its destruction proved to be the end of a dream.

- The Munich air disaster of 1958 killed many of the brightest and best young footballers of that generation. Manchester United had a great team known as the 'Busby babes'. Despite the disaster, Manchester United rose from the ashes and is a great team today.

Escapes

- When the World Trade Center was hit by a terrorist attack on September 11, 2001, a number of people lived to tell the tale.
- The sinking of the SS *Golden Gate* (1862) was as big as the sinking of the *Titanic*. Survivors were able to tell their own stories.
- Apollo 13 was a near space disaster. With the help of ground control, the astronauts managed to escape death and arrive back on Earth.
- The long walk – a group of men walked 4,000 miles to escape from a Soviet labour camp in Siberia.

Mysteries

- What actually happened to the *Mary Celeste?*
- Atlantis, the lost city. Did it ever exist?
- Are there alien spacecraft in the Nevada desert?
- Does Bigfoot exist?
- Are crop circles real or a hoax?

These 'mysteries', however we view them, are fascinating for students and especially the kind of boys who would otherwise not engage with English.

Sporting achievements

- Geoff Hurst's Football World Cup winning hat-trick.
- Muhammed Ali, a boxing legend.
- The Lewis Hamilton story – so far.
- Roger Federer, the greatest male tennis player ever?

Endurance

- Climbing Everest.
- Discovering Australia.
- Ellen MacArthur and the Vendée Globe.

Below is an example of a text that boys will be able to engage with, which is also available online.

The Sinking of the SS *Golden Gate*

The American Civil War raged. Life was dangerous. Some people wanted to leave America, they wanted to get out quickly.

On July 21, 1862, one of the fastest steamers on the West Coast of America left San Francisco. There were 338 passengers and crew, and a great deal of gold aboard ship. The SS *Golden Gate* was heading for Panama and away from the Civil War.

The voyage was never completed and 213 people died when the ship caught fire. It sank off Manzanillo, Mexico.

On the evening of Sunday July 27, people were sitting down for dinner. The ship was 15 miles offshore and the sea was calm. Suddenly, a fire was discovered near the ship's engines. The captain, W.W. Hudson, ordered the ship to make a dash for the shoreline. Smoke poured from the engine room. The SS *Golden Gate* picked up speed and the fire spread.

By about 5pm the ship was still 3 miles from shore. Passengers panicked and began to jump ship. The lifeboats were launched. There were enough lifeboats to save everyone on-board ship. However, many were never filled.

Tragically, the SS *Golden Gate* ran aground 300 yards from the shore.

Of the 134 steerage passengers, only 33 survived.

A young boy named George Fulton was on the ship when it caught fire that day. George was only 7 years old. He was with his uncle and some of his family.

As soon as they knew the ship was on fire, the Fulton family went up on deck. Their uncle urged the young Fulton boys to jump into the water and swim for shore. George's brother, Julius, could not swim and soon drowned. George managed to make it to the shore. He fell down on the beach, exhausted.

The following morning, two men found him. They also found a big sack of potatoes. One man picked up the sack, the other took George by the hand.

The survivors walked for hours under the hot sun. They were seeking rescue. George grew very tired and slumped to the ground. He could go no further.

The men debated as to whether George was worth carrying. They wondered if he would be a burden to them. Eventually, they carried him between them and left the potatoes behind!

After a long trek, they reached the town of Manzanillo. George survived and was adopted by a bachelor uncle. He lived to tell the tale.

What happened to the gold is a mystery. Did it sink with the ship or was it stolen?

Suggested work from the passage

When you have given the students the passage and they have read it, do try the following work that could emerge from it. Try adapting the following suggestions for your groups. I always find it worthwhile to allow students to do some drama work before they attempt any written work. It stimulates their imaginations and they can picture the sequence of events better. The outcome is much improved written work.

- Freeze-framing. Ask students to freeze-frame an important moment from the sinking of the SS *Golden Gate*. (Freeze-framing is where the actors can practise facial expressions/body movements to communicate the thoughts and feelings of those involved in the action.)
- Hot-seating. Ask students, already placed in small groups of about four, to hot-seat the captain, George and a steerage passenger. Ask them about their role in the tragedy. Tell them to keep in character and find supporting evidence from the text, if possible.
- In some cases tell them that they will need to use their imaginations. For example, how did George feel as he watched his brother drown? Why didn't the lifeboats pick up everyone? Why did so many people die when there were enough lifeboat spaces for everyone?
- Allow students to improvise a scene from the sinking of the ship and mime the action.

Do give the students a time limit on these activities. The time limit may depend upon the group. Take care to make sure that they are on task and motivated. When you feel that the students have completed the drama work, you may wish to move them on to written work. I have devised the comprehension passage but do adapt it, depending upon the ability of the group.

Tell the students that in the first three of the following questions, they will need to pick out words and phrases from the passage to back-up their ideas. They could work in pairs on this task or individually. They might need to go through the questions orally or you may like them to look and write down the answers individually. As there are no valid alternative answers in some of the questions, it would be useful to have a class or group debate before any answers are written.

1. How do we know life was dangerous in America in 1862?
2. What does the captain order when he realizes the SS *Golden Gate* is on fire? Do you think his orders were sensible?
3. George's uncle urged the Fulton boys to jump into the water. From your reading of the whole passage, was this a sensible idea?

4. Why do you think the men took George with them rather than the sack of potatoes?
5. Why do you think most of the steerage passengers drowned?
6. Can you see any irony in the sinking of the SS *Golden Gate*?

Following are some creative writing suggestions that should engage the boys' interest. Do adapt and write your own or use my suggestions.

Creative writing

Imagine that you are a survivor of the SS *Golden Gate*, write down your memoirs in diary form. (You could be a steerage passenger, the captain of the ship or a wealthy passenger who is eating a meal as the fire breaks out.)

1. Imagine that you are a passenger. You know there is gold aboard ship. Write your story about your escape from the blazing ship. Did you go for the gold or did you make sure you survived?
2. Imagine that you are George. Describe your experiences as you escape the SS *Golden Gate* and are eventually adopted by your bachelor uncle.

Non-fiction material

Following is a list of three books I would like to recommend on non-fiction work. Two are my own books:

- *Exploring the Extreme* (West, 2003a);
- *Back to the Wild* (West, 2003b);
- *The Real World* (Barton, 1998).

Most students like animals. There are many stories about animals but what of facts written about animals? A boy I taught about 8 years ago was a disaffected Year 8 student. He wrote very little until I asked him about his interests. I discovered that he was brilliant with animals. He knew more about snakes than anyone I knew. Getting him to write about snakes was a revelation. Work on animals might well prove to be popular and the work could improve the students' written and comprehending skills.

Following is one I have used about foxes. This is also available online.

Foxes: fact sheet

The only fox found in Britain is the red fox.

Where foxes live

Foxes live almost anywhere. Many are found in cities and towns but they are also found in woods, forests and rural areas. You are most likely to spot a fox in the evening or at night.

Foxes roam at night in search of food. They are not fussy eaters and they might look in dustbins for the remains of a chicken or they could hunt for voles or rabbits. Foxes also eat beetles, crabs and dead fish or seabirds.

Home life

Although foxes are mostly seen alone, they usually live in small groups. The male is called a dog fox and the female is called a vixen. The couple live with their young cubs and sometimes other vixens, who act as aunts. They live in a den, which could be an abandoned rabbit burrow or a rock crevice.

The whole family is active at night. The cubs play-fight and groom each other. Foxes greet each other by wagging their tails – as dogs do. Foxes usually have four or five cubs. The cubs are born blind and are covered in hair.

Fox tricks

Foxes can climb well, unlike dogs or wolves. They have been spotted sitting in lower branches of trees!

If foxes have eaten well and they want to save extra food for another day, they will bury their food and come back to it when they are hungry.

Five amazing facts about foxes

- Foxes are known to use a wide range of vocal sounds and pitch tones to communicate with each other.
- The Japanese believe the fox is a sacred animal.
- Foxes are the smallest member of the dog family. Although they are members of the dog family, their eyes are cat-like. They also have retractable claws and play with their prey – just as cats do.
- The world's smallest fox is the Fennec fox, which weighs just 1.6kg. Its hearing is so good it can hear its prey moving underground.
- Foxes are found on all the world's continents except Antarctica.

Conclusion

The fox is an interesting animal that can adapt to different environments.

Having given students this passage, you may wish to adapt the suggested work I used with my students. I would ask them to set out a fact sheet about an animal they know something about. Initially, I would ask students to use the internet or to read library books to discover more about an animal or insect that would interest them the most.

Students will then need to set out a fact sheet using the headings below. These are also available online:

- Where the animal lives and hunts.
- Its home life.
- What the animal looks like.
- Five amazing facts.
- A conclusion.

You may ask students to complete the fact sheet, set out as I have in my example (above). They can then use their IT skills to lay it out uniquely and the fact sheet could form part of an interesting classroom display.

You might also want the fact sheet to form the basis of a comprehension exercise, to check on how much the students have understood the work. The comprehension exercise below is quite a simple one and can be used with lower-ability students. This is also available online in case you would like to hand it out to the students.

Foxes

1. Where are foxes most likely to be found?
2. What foods are foxes most likely to eat?
3. What name is given to a female fox?
4. What are foxes able to do that dogs or wolves cannot do?
5. If foxes have food left over, what do they do with it?
6. What do the Japanese think about foxes?
7. Why are foxes like cats?
8. What is interesting about the Fennec fox?
9. Which continent has no foxes?

The fact sheet could also be used as a basis for a vocabulary exercise, as demonstrated below.

Tell the students:

In your own words, explain the following. You may use a dictionary if necessary:

1. fussy;
2. abandoned;
3. active at night;
4. vocal sounds;
5. pitch tones;
6. communicate;
7. sacred;
8. retractable claws;
9. continent;
10. environment.

The words above are available online so you can hand them out to the students.

Draw before you write

Some students are able to write more effectively and with greater imagination if they are given the chance to draw their ideas. They need to be aware that their drawings do not need to be good, and that they will not gain extra marks for their drawings. They are taking part in an English lesson and not an art lesson.

When students are given a title for their story, they may want to storyboard the events first. The way to do this is to fold a piece of paper into about eight squares. Students then plan their story, drawing what happens in each square. Underneath the eight drawings, students need to write about the action taking place in a sentence of their own writing. In reality, this is no more than planning a story and making sure things follow a sequence of events. However, some students do feel that following a drawing of events improves their written work.

Two other tasks that allow students to draw and write are: inventing new planets and writing to persuade.

A new planet – Silvershine

Ask students to imagine that the year is 2090. Planet Earth is in trouble. Global warming has taken its toll. Food is running out and water is hard to find. The only hope for mankind is to discover a new planet that can support human life.

Captain Granger and his crew have been asked to explore Planet Silvershine. They need to report back to Earth and discover if the planet can sustain human life. The captain has to send a daily log back to Earth, electronically.

Tell students that you are going to read out an extract from the captain's log. He is writing about all he saw as his spacecraft landed on Planet Silvershine. This is also available online.

> We had a smooth landing on Planet Silvershine. The sky is very blue and there are fluffy white clouds in the sky, just like on Earth. We are all feeling very warm. Perhaps we have landed in a place like Australia in the summer. There are no desert areas here, though. The grass is green, so the planet must have rain.
>
> Outside the spacecraft, the soil is much like Earth soil. In the distance, the mountain tops appear as if they are tipped with silver. They look like teeth with fillings. Most of the mountains are brown and barren. Some of the mountains have dark shadows and we think they could be hollow and there might be caves.
>
> We have all noticed some strange plants among the green grass. They are bright yellow and appear like little suns . . . but they move when we look at them. Our doctor has knick-named them the 'dancing flowers'.

Not too far away there are tall slim trees. They look as if they are full of orange fruit. Each fruit is as big as a melon.

What to do

- Tell students to list four facts that they have discovered by reading Captain Granger's log.
- As crew members, they can name the various mountains, trees and the two different plants that are mentioned.
- Students can draw what they think the planet looks like, after re-reading the captain's log. They will need plain paper for this exercise.
- Students can imagine that they are Captain Granger and can write one or two paragraphs describing other plants and trees that Captain Granger has seen. Are there rivers, seas, sand and different types of food on the planet?

Continuing

If you wish to take this exercise further, you can read the second log from Captain Granger's account. This is also available online. A week has passed by and the captain and his crew have discovered many new things.

When my team and I were out exploring, we discovered that the moving yellow plants are not plants at all. They are small living creatures who only 'come out' when the sun shines. They do not appear afraid of us and they come quite close, making squeaking noises. They blink in the sun and their eyes are as brown as boot polish. I've instructed my men not to touch them or harm them in any way.

We now know there is life on the planet.

We trekked towards the mountains but only got to within about 5 miles of them. We came across a fast-flowing stream. Andrews, one of my bravest men, placed a foot in the water. Three large fish with shark-like teeth tried to bite his big toe. This appears strange, but I'm sure they tried to grab his toe with their tiny black hands. Perhaps they are giant tadpoles? Andrews was quick to get his foot out of the water.

We were about to turn back when we heard a noise coming from the mountains. The sound was like the beating of drums. We might be in trouble!

Continuing further

Ask students to work out what they think might happen next.

- They are sent from Earth to find out what has happened to Captain Granger and his crew. Mission Control has not heard from him for 2 weeks.
- They discover Captain Granger's damaged log. The pages are torn and the spacecraft is ruined. All that can be read are the following words:

Mountains Caves Creatures
Spies Weapons Surrounded

Ask the students to storyboard what might have happened to the captain and his crew. Say to them, 'Use the clues to help you.'

Students can, if they wish, write a log describing how they rescued the captain and his crew from the enemy in the caves. They can storyboard their ideas first.

Persuasion

The idea is for students to look at how language is used to persuade and encourage people to buy a certain product, or to alter their opinion about a person or an issue. In the example I give below, the task is to persuade others to spend their money! The story is also available online.

Fear World – meet your fears!
Enter at your peril

- What lurks in the dungeons? Dare you go and discover the dungeon's secrets?
- Be brave – follow the fear trail . . . from the French Revolution to meeting the most notorious murderers in history.
- Scary rides – dare you have a go?
- Meet the Sabre-toothed tiger and other beasts. You thought they were extinct!
- Scale the highest tower in the world.
- Spend 20 minutes locked up with spiders and other creepy crawlies.
- Visit cliff-hanger way.
- Go back in time to a Victorian school, to a time when teachers were very scary.
- Get stuck in a lift.
- Become trapped down a mine.

Also featured:

- Our award-winning adventure playground.
- Tea rooms.

Christine and Robert Dunwell welcome you to their twelfth season in charge of Fear World.

The theme park is set in 30 acres of country park, just outside
Basingstoke. This is still the premier attraction in Hampshire.
A really wonderful experience for all the family.
Here, you will know real fear. You will want to run away – but
there is nowhere to go!
Real actors are used in the theme park. They may go near you but
they won't touch you!

Comments:
'We couldn't drag the kids away. We were here until the park
closed.'
Alice Smethhurst, Birmingham

'Bad weather is no bother. Many of the activities are indoors.'
Mr Patel, London

'Even the tots loved it. There is something for all the family.'
Jacob Webb, Kempshott

'Everyone loves this theme park and there is plenty to do. The
Grim Reaper restaurant has daily specials and offers smaller,
cheaper meals for the young and the very old.'
Wendy Smith, Brighton

'There are food options for vegetarians and diabetics. Many
choices are nut free.'
Pembe Constantinou, London

Activities

- Ask the students to design a leaflet for Fear World. To model
  how leaflets are set out, bring some examples into the
  classroom; most tourist information centres will oblige. The
  students will need to think about headlines, small paragraphing
  and illustrations/drawings. They can add to the information
  if they wish. For example, they could mention there is a new
  toilet block which is designed with disabled people in mind.
- Allow the students to work in pairs and study the advert for
  Fear World. They should then jot down all there is to see and
  do there.
- They should consider if the style of the leaflet is meant to be
  serious, jokey, factual, friendly or informal.
- Is the leaflet easy to read? Will it help to attract customers?
  What types of people are most likely to visit the theme park?
- Ask them to read what people who have visited the theme
  park have to say. Are the quotes effective in persuading
  people to visit Fear World?
- Students can then choose three sentences from the leaflet that

they believe will make people want to visit the theme park. They should then give reasons for their choice.

Then tell the students the following:

- Imagine a theme park has been designated for your village or town. Its aim is to attract as many people as possible. You have been asked to design a leaflet to attract people to the new theme park. Before you begin, some decisions have to be made.
- Work in groups and decide upon the name of your new theme park. What will be the theme? What attractions will you offer? How will they differ from what is on offer in existing theme parks? What facilities will you offer?
- For a full day out, you will need to provide toilets and a wide choice of food and drinks.

Tell the students:

- How will you lay out your leaflet? Decide on headings, titles and subtitles to make your leaflet look professional.
- What artwork or drawings will you include in your leaflet?
- Slogans are words or phrases that stick in the mind. They are usually short and they capture the reader's attention. You could use some in your leaflet.

Following are two examples:

1. Frightening and Fearful Fun.
2. Cross the Creaky Cool Bridge of Doom.

As a teacher, you may wish to talk to the students about alliteration at this point.

Tell the students that they now need to design their own leaflet. Points to emphasize are:

- You might wish to include some slogans in your leaflet.
- You might want to experiment with your leaflet.
- Go for a strong visual image with catchy headlines.
- You need to capture the attention of the buying public.
- Think about short paragraphs, use of bullet points, font style, types of headings and subheadings. You might want to experiment with typeface.

What have the students learned?
They have learned how to:

- use persuasive language and how language can be persuasive;

- use bullet points;
- use short paragraphs for effect;
- design a leaflet;
- use headings and subheadings.

The students will have produced something to be proud of, which looks good. They will have either drawn images on the leaflet or used computer-generated images.

I have discovered that most Years 7–9 students enjoy this exercise. Learning becomes fun and a good piece of work is produced at the end of the task. Do use the leaflets as part of your classroom display.

Writing reviews

To teach students how to write reviews, the best way in is to tap into the students' interests. Writing a music review is a good idea, as the vast majority of students know something about pop stars.

As a starter, ask the students to give their opinions about a band or a pop star they feel they know something about. You might get responses such as:

I think _____ _____ are the best band because their music appeals to my age group. They are a hip-hop group from Coventry and they sing about things that really matter to me.

Or

In my opinion _____ _____ is the best pop singer in the country. I really like what she's doing right now. I think she'll be really big very soon.

There is not a lot of substance to the above examples of a review. One way to produce better work is to ask the students to review an album song by song, or for them to pick out four different songs in the album. The other way is to ask them to find out as much information as they can about their chosen band or singer. This will enable them to write a more informed review. The students should be allowed to research the internet or pop magazines so that the reviews move away from vague opinions. They might come up with something like the example below.

Rollercoaster

Rollercoaster formed in March 2008. They wanted to popularize Country music and bring it into the twenty-first century by using a faster beat. They originally performed cover versions, which became almost heavy metal under their playing. People of all ages loved the sound and, by January 2009, they had brought out their own album. Their original soundtracks, such as 'Breaking my Heart, Babe', stormed to number one in the UK charts. They were working on their second album when lead singer, Ashley Grantchester, was struck down with a mystery illness.

CHAPTER 5

Making the assessment focus work

Tackling the assessment focus

The assessment focus is really divided into writing and reading. Looking at the assessment focus regarding writing, I shall endeavour to show you how students can improve their writing by using the AFs to improve their work.

AF1 Write imaginative, interesting and thoughtful texts

Writing from real experience can bring a student's writing alive. If students can actually picture or relive an incident that has taken place in their lives, their writing will show good detail.

Following is an example of writing from real experience. This is also available online:

> Mr Manton was the strangest teacher I have ever known. He was also our form teacher.
>
> Harry Manton was a small, plump man who sat at his wooden desk and peered over it like a toad having a nervous breakdown. He always dressed in a brown tracksuit, which heightened his toad-like appearance.
>
> In form time, he barked out our names as if he was an army officer and we were all on parade.
>
> Manton also taught games. Once a week, he'd carry a heavy rucksack into the changing rooms. He'd tell us boys we were going on a cross-country run. This would be followed by the usual groans and moans and production of excuse notes. He'd tell us the route, blow his whistle and see us all off. Then we'd see him carrying his rucksack in the direction of town.
>
> One day we followed him and noticed he'd gone into the launderette. His clothes were taken out of the rucksack and all placed into a washing

machine. Then he'd head back into school – ready for our return. No doubt the following class would also have to run a cross-country route while he collected his washing!

Why the headteacher allowed Manton to do this, we'll never know.
Andy Leeson

Tell the students to look at the following, which are also available online:

- With a partner, find one detail from the passage that really sticks in your mind.
- In pairs, find other details from the passage that you believe are well written.
- In pairs, discuss how the passage could be improved. Perhaps there should be more description or more use of metaphors and similes?
- Write about somebody you know well. Think about any strange or unusual habits they might have. Think about an incident that involves that person. How can you make it 'come alive' for the reader?

The students should write an interesting story from their own experience.

AF2 *Produce texts that are appropriate to task, reader and purpose*
The students are going to write a tourist leaflet about their town or village. They will need to write a paragraph that will persuade visitors to be attracted to their area. They need to know the following:

- They are to write a persuasive text.
- They will be writing for people they don't know, so they will need to write formally.
- Their writing needs to appeal to a wide range of people and a varied age range.
- They need to describe the attractions in their area.

Ask the students to look at the example below. This is also available online:

Harford is a pretty village in Cambridgeshire. There is a main street going right through this long village.

Although a small place, this village has two shops. One shop is a hairdressers and the other is a general store, selling all types of food. There is also a pub, which serves meals on a Saturday and bar snacks the rest of the week.

There is a village pond, which is full of small fish.

Harford is a good place to visit.
Graham Bentworth

Ask the students the following question:

Do you think the description above would persuade people to visit Harford? Why? Why not?

The students should work out that the description is not particularly persuasive and unlikely to attract visitors of all ages to the area. Harford sounds like many other places. This should show students that they need to choose a place near them that has quite a few attractions and gives them something to write about. If they do live in a small village, they might need to write about their nearest town or large village.

They should now look at the example below. This is also available online:

Great Coverley is an amazing place. Why don't you visit our fantastic village? There is something for everyone here.

Do visit our famous market, which takes place every alternate Friday in the month. When the market is in full swing during the summer months, there are street entertainers, jugglers, singers and street artists. The French market occurs the first week in June and the third week in September. So come along for a crêpe or some French cheese.

There is a wide range of shops, selling almost everything you will ever need.

Food? There is an authentic Mexican restaurant, two wonderful Indian restaurants and a classy Italian place. The two village pubs serve generous helpings of traditional English dishes. The Queen's Head has a steak night every Saturday.

Great Coverley boasts a multiplex cinema nearby and there is an out of town ice skating rink and bowling complex within driving distance of the village.

Why not relax by the river? You can hire boats from Little Coverley, a village just along the road. Then you can row into our village and moor near The Queen's Head.

October is now our famous scarecrow week, which was set up by the Millennium Committee but has been an annual event ever since.

Whatever you're into and whatever your age, there is something for you at Great Coverley.

Chloe Greenish

Ask the students to find examples of how the writer has engaged the reader, chosen interesting descriptive words and started her sentences in a variety of ways.

Although not strictly formal, Chloe has interested the reader and made people of all ages want to visit the area in which she lives.

As a writing task, students can think about the area they live in. They will need to describe it in an attractive way, so that people will want to visit the area.

AF3 *Organize and present whole texts effectively*

The task for the students is to divide a plain piece of paper into eight. They can then plan their own comic strip. They will need to draw the action in their eight strips and write either dialogue or action in each strip. The words should be kept brief for this activity. They should plan each frame before they begin to draw or write anything.

Below is a bank of ideas for possible plots:

- alien invasion;
- a robbery;
- lost in the mountains;
- war in outer space;
- robots take over;
- the other world;
- a kidnap.

You might like the students to develop this idea further by writing their story and making sure the paragraphs in the story follow on in a logical way.

If the students need a model, you can ask them to look at this example. The eight strips could have had the following words beneath them:

1. Matt Hardy and his son looked into the night sky.
2. A spaceship shot through the sky and landed in Matt's field.
3. Matt and Tom (his son) saw grey aliens walk from the spaceship.
4. Other spaceships shot through the sky and landed in the cornfields.
5. The grey aliens were meeting in the field.
6. Now the aliens were marching like an army.
7. Matt telephoned the police. They contacted the army.
8. Army planes were destroying the enemy spaceships.

The story

Now the students have written their comic strips, they can go on to write the story. Following is an example to give them, which also is available on the internet, before they start. It is just the beginning of the story and has only used the first comic strip. Point out that we get dad's reasons for star gazing and also Tom's reason.

Matt yawned and put down his newspaper. His favourite football team had lost again. Relegation loomed! He wanted to do something to take his mind off the game. As a young boy, he'd been thrilled when his dad took him outside to gaze up at the night stars. It was a cold, frosty evening. Ideal for star gazing. Couldn't he share the experience with his son?

Matt shouted upstairs, 'Tom, let's do something different!'

Tom switched off his music player. 'Yeah, whatever, dad.'

'No, really, Tom. I want to show you some of life's wonders.'

Tom ran downstairs wondering what bee his dad now had in his bonnet. Last week it was an all-night fishing trip that ended up with no fish and a soaking when the leaking boat eventually sank. He didn't want to curb his dad's enthusiasm, so he decided to comply.

Matt took Tom into the garden.

'Look up at the sky, Tom. Look at all the billions of stars out there. They're all different suns. Have you ever wondered about the vastness of space?'

Now ask the students to complete the story.

AF4 Construct paragraphs and use cohesion

Point out to students that there are different reasons for starting new paragraphs in a story. These are:

- a change of speaker;
- a change of place;
- a change of time;
- a change of topic.

Look at the following extract from *Lost on the Mountains*. This is also available online.

I glanced at Dave. I could tell he was thinking the same as me.

'We're lost, aren't we?'

Dave nodded. 'It's the mist. It's so thick. Can't see a thing.'

I remembered another time with Dave. I recalled a day 5 years back. His mother had just died. He'd walked out of the big hospital doors. He had a funny expression on his face, a kind of twisted nervous grin.

He was wearing the same expression now. That's how I knew we were in trouble.

Ask the students to point out where the writer has used a new paragraph for a change of speaker, place, time and topic in this short extract.

Using a title from the AF3 examples, ask the students to write a short extract using a new paragraph for a change of speaker, place, time and topic. They might be able to combine more than one in just one paragraph. For example, in the above extract a change of time, place and topic occurred in one paragraph.

Time – 5 years back.

Place – out of the big hospital doors.

Topic – mother had just died.

AF5 *Vary sentences for clarity, purpose and effect*

Ask the students to look at the following passage, which is also available online.

> The night stalker was in the graveyard. Then he sat next to a grave. Then he heard footsteps. Then he licked his lips. Then he was ready for his next victim.

Point out that, although the story could become exciting, it reads as average writing. All the writer can hope for is a level four. The sentences all sound the same and the word 'then' is overused.

Tell the students that connectives are useful in that they can make the writing much more interesting.

Examples of connectives are:

> As After Although Because Since Until While Where

Tell the students that if they wish to change a simple sentence into a complex sentence and add more detail, they will make the story sound much better and more professional, thus raising their level.

> While the nightstalker was in the graveyard there was fear in the town. Whenever he sat next to a grave there would be trouble.

It is also effective to vary the sentence length, as shown below and also available online.

> He heard footsteps. He licked his lips. Now he was ready for his next victim.

Ask the students to write a paragraph or two using connectives and varying their sentence length. The topic could be from the list of suggestions for AF3.

AF6 *Write with technical accuracy of syntax and punctuation*

Students need to present speech accurately, to move them on to a higher level. Using speech correctly will also be part of the functional skills assessment in English at GCSE.

You will need to make students aware that speech marks go around the actual words of a speaker. Any punctuation in the speech goes inside the speech marks. Also, if the speaker breaks off a sentence in a speech, this can be shown in two different ways, they are:

- by an ellipsis (. . .);
- or a dash (–).

Following are examples to show the students, which are also available online:

> 'We need to get ready,' said Deepal.
>
> 'Why?' asked Linda.

'We're going swimming,' said Deepal.

'But . . . I can't swim,' answered Linda.

'I didn't know you couldn't swim – you never told me,' said Deepal.

As an exercise, ask the students to punctuate the following, which is also available online:

We should climb this mountain by nightfall said Gareth

The really high mountain on the horizon asked Megan

Yes the high one in the distance answered Gareth

You're joking . . . I'm not climbing that exclaimed Megan

I thought you were up for a real challenge – obviously you're not said Gareth

There is also an online resource for punctuation and the use of clauses.

AF7 Select appropriate and effective vocabulary

To enhance students' work, they need to be aware of the use of adjectives and adverbs.

Remind the students that adjectives are used to describe nouns. (Nouns are people, places and things.) Note that adjectives can modify (describe) nouns. Examples are:

- *Very* old and *slightly* mad.
- The *hot* breeze.

Adverbs describe verbs. (Verbs are doing or being words.) An example would be, 'the hot breeze blew *relentlessly*'.

Ask the students to work in pairs and replace the blanks with an adjective or with an adverb in the following story, which is also available online. The story is about a detective entering a disused warehouse.

The _____ detective walked into the _____ warehouse. There was an _____ of wind. The icy wind blew _____.

The detective reacted _____. He heard a _____ voice. He shouted _____. There was a _____ silence. He strode down the long _____ corridor. He entered the _____ room. He held his gun _____. There was a deep and _____ silence. Nobody was in the _____ room. The _____ criminals had fled.

AF8 Use correct spelling

It is worth reminding the students about the use of plurals. For most words, just adding the letter 's' will turn singular into plural words.

Cat – Cats
Window – Windows

If the singular noun ends in an 'f', it needs to be changed into a 'v' before adding an 'es' and changing it into a plural word.

Thief – Thieves
Leaf – Leaves

Ask the students to think of five more plural words that use the 'f' into a 'v' rule.

Looking at the assessment focus regarding reading, I aim to show you how the students can maintain motivation through interesting and exciting work.

AF2 Understand, describe, select or retrieve information, events and ideas from texts and use quotation and reference to texts

---

The Wessex News – *A Deserved Victory*

Wessex 2   v.   **Dorchester 1**
Duncans 52   Wells 45
Mills (pen. 90)

Wessex beat local rivals Dorchester by a deserved 2–1 victory, to put them top of the Hardy Memorial League.

Dorchester started the match sluggishly. Their game plan was to come away with a draw. They hacked at everything that moved and Troy Copitch was lucky not to see red early on, when he felled Tony Duncans.

The negative Dorchester side frustrated the home team time and again by packing their penalty box with ten men.

On the stroke of half-time and against the run of play, Wells scored a lucky break-away goal. A tame left-footed shot hit the post and dribbled over the goal-line.

Our superb Wessex side dominated the second half, with manager Henchard urging them on from the touchline. Justice was done when Tony Duncans scored in a packed penalty box. The score was now level and Wessex continued to press for the winner.

When the game appeared to be heading for a draw, Troy Copitch brought down young Scott Farfrey, who had worked hard on the wing all afternoon. This time, Copitch did see red and was promptly dispatched for an early shower. Captain Brian Mills scored from the penalty spot.

Wessex will be deserving champions if they win the last match of the season against Corfe United next Saturday.

Dorchester Daily – *We Were Robbed*

Wessex 2 v. **Dorchester 1**
Duncans 52   Wells 45
Mills (pen. 90)

The referee, Joe Mears, needs glasses. Dorchester played a canny defensive game that should have paid off.

Gordon Well's superb strike, on the stroke of half-time, had the Wessex goalie stranded on his line: Wessex 0, Dorchester 1. That should have been the final result. Unfortunately, Mr Mears had other ideas on his mind as he headed for his half-time rest.

On 52 minutes, Duncans received a pass from team mate Hugh Bates. The pass was blatantly offside. The only players in the penalty area when he received the ball were the Dorchester team. That goal should never have been allowed.

Brave Dorchester held on, with a stout and resolute defensive display.

Just before the final whistle was blown, Troy Copitch tapped Scott Farfray's ankle and the Wessex player was rolling on the ground as if pole-axed. The biased referee immediately ordered a penalty without consulting a linesman.

We ask the question, why was any extra time allowed? There were no injury stoppages! Why was the penalty awarded? This match has robbed Dorchester of the championship title. No doubt about it, we were robbed.

The trick with this assessment focus is to find an interesting passage that will stimulate the students. Try this one! It is interesting to compare texts. Ask the students to read the reports of the same football match from the point of view of two different newspapers. These are also available online.

Ask the students to read the two newspaper accounts and then list the differences between them. They should bring the following to your attention:

- One newspaper's headline is 'A Deserved Victory' and the other states, 'We Were Robbed'.

Wessex:
- The Dorchester player, Troy Capitch, could have been sent off early on.
- Dorchester played in a negative way.
- Wells scored a lucky goal, against the run of play.
- Tony Duncan's penalty meant justice was done.

Dorchester:
- Play was described as canny, rather than negative.
- The referee was blamed for poor decisions.
- Wells' goal was described as a 'superb strike'.
- The equalizer was claimed to be offside.
- The penalty decision was controversial.

As an extra activity, ask the students to write a biased account of a recent sporting event. If possible, find different newspaper accounts of the same event.

AF3 *Deduce, infer or interpret information, events or ideas from texts*

Ask the students to work in pairs and look at the review from a story called *No Name* by Wilkie Collins (1862). Tell them Collins was writing in the nineteenth century. Tell them to bullet point five things they think the novel will be about. This extract is also available online.

A review of *No Name* by Wilkie Collins

This is one of Wilkie Collins' underrated novels. The heroine, Magdaline Vanstone, and her sister are disinherited when their father is killed in a train crash.

Family secrets are uncovered, such as the Vanstone daughter's illegitimacy and the family's fall from society.

Collins' novel is subversive in that it attacks Victorian laws. His heroine is modern in appeal as she shows determination in the way that she attempts to get back all that she feels belongs to her.

As an activity, ask the students to write a review of a book they have read recently, or a film they have seen lately.

Now ask them to look at the start of a modern story called *At the Gate*. This is also available online.

At the Gate

Stuart peered out of his bedroom window. At the bottom of the garden stood the young fair-haired woman he'd seen before. The one who looked so much like his own mother, except her hair was as golden as wheat in late summer. Except her eyes were as blue as the ocean. Otherwise, he could have been looking out at his own mother as she might have been before he was born.

The soldier was brushing dust off his uniform as he marched quickly along the narrow lane to the gate where the young woman stood waiting for him. The soldier reached her and they held hands. They walked together back the way the soldier had come from. Two lovers, holding hands, happy. They stopped outside Stuart's bedroom window and looked up at him. They smiled straight at him, the American soldier winked.

But how could that be? The house wasn't built in 1945. The lane does not exist now, in the year 2009. How could they both see him?

Stuart shivered. He **knew** they'd seen him. The couple looked straight at him and walked on down the lane that was fading into a ground mist.

Ask the students to work out what appear to be the main themes and issues in the novel so far. Who do they think will be the main characters? What might happen next?

They may be surprised to discover that the novel is a murder mystery with a difference. The young woman and her soldier went missing in 1945 and most people at the time assumed they had eloped to America.

Students can now look at the second extract, which is taken from the middle of the novel. This is also available online.

At the Gate (middle)

So, my great aunt Martha did not elope. She was murdered and her lifeless body was thrust down this well,' said Stuart, as he gazed into its murky depths.

Augustina shrugged her delicate shoulders.

'We don't know that the body belonged to her. There will need to be DNA tests, or something . . . won't there?'

Stuart peered down the dark and deep well. He almost felt the well would give him all the answers to all the questions he wanted to ask. His great-aunt's body had been down the well for almost seventy years.

'I want to find out the truth. I want to know what really happened all those years ago.'

Augustina laughed.

'It's obvious. The Yank killed her and hoofed it quickly back to his own country. He's probably dead himself now. Oh, Stuart, let sleeping dogs lie!'

Stuart picked at a root of grass, twiddling a stalk between his index finger and his thumb. 'The dreams, it's as if they're trying to tell me something. Both of them!'

Augustina laughed again, 'Nobody will remember anything. And those that might, won't talk.'

'There's your great-grandma. She's still alive and she's lived in the village all her life. She still has all her faculties – you said so yourself.'

Augustina shivered. She felt cold, as if a dark cloud had passed over her.

'Let bygones be bygones,' she heard herself say.

Stuart peered down the well for the last time. When his friend looked down at him, she could see the determination in his eyes, in his body. She knew she had no choice. She had to help this boy who'd come into her life.

Ask students to work in pairs and bullet point the main events in this extract. They then need to write a few lines on each of the two characters, mentioning what they know about each one.

As an additional exercise, ask the students to finish the story in a page or two of their own writing.

AF4 Identify and comment on the structure and organization of texts
Ask the students to read the following piece of writing. This is also available online.

A Visit to Colchester

We got off the coach and it was raining. We split up into groups. Mr Ballard and Miss Tomlin led our group. We looked around the shops. I got bored and was told off for playing football with a tin can. Then we went into a cafe and I ate pie and chips and left the peas. I had a drink. I heard the rain last night as it bounced off the shed roof. I thought it'd rain today. I got up early this morning and had a shower. I then watched television while I ate breakfast. I got annoyed with my sister because she hogged the shower and she knew I didn't want to be late for the school trip. It stopped raining so we went out of the cafe and walked to the park. There was a ruin of a Roman wall. There was also a lake. Then we listened to a talk about the Romans. Last year we did Henry VIII in history but he was a Tudor. He wasn't a Roman. After the park, we walked to the coach and later we got back to school. It was a good day. Oh, yeah, we went to these special gardens and then we went to the seaside after the park.
By Grant Easton

Ask the students the following questions:

- Could you work out what Grant had done?
- What detail could have been added?
- What could have been missed out?
- Was it easy or difficult to follow? Why?

Tell the students that the piece of writing needs restructuring. It also needs to be written using paragraphs. Events need to be written as they happened.

- Students should be able to re-write the piece for Grant, thinking about the sequence of events and making it sound more exciting. They will have to use their imaginations for the seaside and the gardens.
- Ask the students to write about a place they have visited recently, make it sound interesting so that other people would like to visit that place.

AF5 Explain and comment on the writer's use of language

Tell the students that the correct use of similes can enhance their work. Remind them that a simile is a comparison. Similes compare one thing with another.

Allow students to read the passage below and pick out the similes. They should spot eight similes. To compare one thing with another, similes use 'as' or 'like'. This text is also available online.

Lord Dimwit

Lord Dimwit's nose was as long as a garden hose. It sniffed out trouble like a bloodhound after a clue. Lord Dimwit could smell the pong of unwashed armpits. There was somebody in his garden. He was being burgled! Lord

Dimwit was on the case like a new Sherlock Holmes.

There was a ladder propped up against the wall of his mansion. A man, looking as suspicious as a fox around hens, was climbing up the ladder.

Lord Dimwit's long nose twitched like a snake at a circus. The man was carrying a bucket and mop.

'Is the man going to steal all my precious gold and silver and put it all in that cheap plastic bucket?' asked Dimwit, talking to himself like a vicar at a tea party.

The ladder slipped and the man wobbled. He fell like a jelly sliding from a plate.

Lord Dimwit ran to the fallen man.

'Are you alright, my fine fellow?' asked Dimwit.

The man got up from the ground, rubbing his bruises.

'I'll be as right as rain,' he said. 'Falling off ladders is part of a window cleaner's job!'

Ask the students which similes in the passage work and which are overdone. Then ask them to choose two similes from the passage and comment on what they are comparing. Or they can make a chart as per the example below:

Subject/object used for comparison

Subject	Object
Dimwit's nose	Garden hose

AF6 Identify and comment on the writer's purposes and viewpoints, and the overall effect of the text on a reader

Wimbledon 2009

Another season in full swing and more British disappointment. Only one Brit left in the last 32 yet again!

The Lawn Tennis Association (LTA) spends up to a reported 24 million a year on player development, with very little return. The last Brit in did not even follow the system! Why is all that money spent with no reward?

The answer, in my opinion, is that the whole Wimbledon tennis thing is too middle class and needs a radical overhaul to bring it into the twenty-first century.

For example, my son and I forced ourselves to rise early and board one of the first early morning trains for London. We eventually arrived in a dangerously packed tube train at Southfields. We couldn't disembark for a while as the station was too crowded. We arrived outside the Wimbledon courts around 11.30am. We were told by a friendly stewardess that we'd be lucky to get in to see any play until 5.30 that evening, too late for our return journey home. Perhaps I was naive. But hang on a minute – as a member of Joe Public could

I buy tickets next time? The stewardess told me that I can't buy tickets in advance, as these are block sold. Well, who gets the tickets?

I could camp out all night and have priority to purchase tickets in the morning.

No wonder the right young people aren't inspired to become the new Roger Federer or the new Venus Williams!

Back to criticism of the British players. There has been criticism from within that the players are all part of a nice, cosy little club. One particular underperformer had eight wildcards on eight consecutive years – and did not win a single game. There is a young and talented girl from Stockport, who has made more progress than any other player this year, who is begging for sponsorship because she can't get onto the next level without money to travel to tournaments abroad. Why can't she have part of that pot of gold? Is tennis an elitist London and Home Counties thing?

May I humbly suggest that the LTA scouts all schools in all areas of the country and searches the predominantly working-class areas, where most footballers come from.

The youngsters with talent should be picked and developed. They should be told from the onset that they have until the age of 18 to break into the top 100, or they are out. Brutal? Competitive? Yes! This method would make them play for their lives. It would find British winners. After all, footballers who underperform are out! Can you imagine the top Premiership teams happy with a bunch of well-spoken underperformers? No! If Manchester United, Chelsea or Liverpool players don't produce the goods, they are sold.

Modern tennis in Britain needs to engage the public, allocate tickets fairly and make players work hard for a living. At present it appears that only one male player gives his all!

By Jeremy Walters

Students should briefly state the viewpoint of the article and list the main points of the argument. They should ask themselves if the case is well argued or could it have been structured more effectively? They should argue that the viewpoint of the writer suggests that the Lawn Tennis Association spends a great deal of money for very little return, in terms of British tennis success. The article is also available online.

The writer also suggests that the Wimbledon event is too middle class and that is partly why British tennis is not successful in attracting the right talent. They may note the following points:

- Tennis in Britain needs a radical overhaul.
- Tennis players in Britain appear to be part of a 'cosy little club'.
- The LTA should scout schools in working-class areas, searching for talent.
- Players should be told to get into the top 100 by a certain age or leave.

- Tickets need to be allocated in a different way.
- Most students will believe the case is well argued.
- Statistics are used (24 million a year on player development).
- The writer uses examples from his own experience.
- The 'cosy little club' is backed up by the example of the girl from Stockport, who does not get the money.
- Practical suggestions for improvement are cited, 'search predominately working-class areas'.
- Comparisons are made with successful football clubs.
- Some students may note that the article is one person's opinion and may not be true. How do we know that the LTA is not scouting all working-class areas, for example. Who is the girl from Stockport? We do not know the reasons behind her lack of funding. Are tickets allocated in the way the writer of the article suggests? Is the article showing bias?

As an additional exercise, students should be encouraged to write an argument on something they feel strongly about. For example, the war in Iraq, global warming, the use of pesticides in farming leading to the death of the honey bee. All these would make good essays.

AF7 Relate texts to their social, cultural and historical traditions

Read students an adapted extract from *Woman in White* by Wilkie Collins (1860). This is also available online in case you would like to display it, or hand it out to some of the students.

Walter Hartright is mentioning his Italian friend named Pesca.

Without being actually a dwarf – for he was perfectly well proportioned from head to foot – Pesca was, I think, the smallest human being I ever saw out of a show-room. Remarkable anywhere, by his personal appearance, he was still further distinguished among the rank and file of mankind by the harmless eccentricity of his character. The ruling idea of his life appeared to be, that he was bound to show his gratitude to the country which had afforded him an asylum and a means of subsistence by doing his utmost to turn himself into an Englishman.

Finding us distinguished, as a nation, by our love of athletic exercises, the little man in the innocence of his heart, devoted himself impromptu to all our English sports and pastimes whenever he had the opportunity of joining them; firmly persuaded that he could adopt our national amusements of the field by an effort of will precisely as he had adopted our national gaiters and our national white hat.

I had seen him risk his limbs blindly at a fox-hunt and in a cricket field; and soon afterwards I saw him risk his life, just as blindly, in the sea at Brighton.

I should have looked after Pesca carefully; but as foreigners are generally quite as well able to take care of themselves in the water as Englishmen, it never occurred to me that the art of swimming might merely add one more to the list of manly exercises which the Professor believed that he could learn impromptu. Soon after we struck out from shore, I stopped, finding my friend did not gain on me, and turned round to look for him. To my horror and amazement, I saw nothing between me and the beach but two little white arms which struggled for an instant above the surface of the water, and then disappeared from view.

Ask the students when they believe this extract was published:
A) 2005 B) 1920 C) 1789 D) 1860 E) 1066?

The extract was from 1860 and was set in the Victorian age. Ask the students what clues are there to suggest that this is part of a Victorian novel. Ask them to look at the author's word choices. Are the words modern? Which ones would not be used in a novel published this year? What social, cultural and historical differences does this novel show? For example, examine the author's thoughts on foreigners. Students should pick out a number of words which they believe are Victorian. The words chosen should form an interesting discussion. The social, cultural and historical differences are wide. For example, Pesca is seen as a comic figure. He must conform to the Victorian view of what an Italian is like. He wishes to turn himself into an Englishman, which reinforces the Victorian view that the English are superior. Remind students that this writing was published before the two World Wars and when Britain had a large empire. Historically, upper-class Englishmen wore gaiters and white hats. Fox hunting and cricket playing were popular pastimes.

Working in pairs, ask the students to answer the following questions:

- Where does Pesca come from?
- What does Pesca look like?
- How does Pesca try to become an Englishman?
- What happened to Pesca at Brighton?

As an additional exercise, allow the students to research the library and pick out a novel written in Victorian times, a novel written in the 1920s and a modern novel, written since 2000. They should read the first two pages of each novel and suggest a difference in how they are written. Are there any cultural and historical differences? What are the social differences?

I have done this particular exercise with top Year 9 students.

CHAPTER 6

Mostly drama

Mysteries

Students enjoy reading and writing about mysteries. There are all sorts of topics for them to read and write about. These include the Loch Ness Monster, the Yeti, Bigfoot, crop circles, Atlantis, the Bermuda Triangle and, the old favourite, the mystery of the *Mary Celeste*. Students' writing improves if they write about something that interests them. Doing their own research gives them 'ownership' of the task.

If you feel that you would like something more teacher directed, try the following.

Read the students the following story of the *Mary Celeste*.

The *Mary Celeste*

One of the greatest mysteries of all times is the story of the *Mary Celeste*. The small ship was found wandering and ghost-like between the Azores and the coast of Portugal. There was nobody on board.

The *Mary Celeste* was an American sailing ship. It set out to cross the Atlantic in November 1872. The ship was taking a cargo of raw alcohol to Italy.

The captain's name was Benjamin Briggs. His family and a small crew were on board.

Three weeks later, a British ship found the *Mary Celeste*. There was nobody on board and it was 650 kilometres from land.

Nobody from the ship was ever seen or heard of again. The mystery of their disappearance has never been solved.

There have been many theories about the abandoned ship.

Give the students the theories and then ask them, in small groups, to work out which one they think is the correct theory. They then need to defend their decision to the rest of the class. The lesson could end with a whole-class debate and vote. The theories are also available online.

Theory One
The sailors might have drunk the cargo of raw alcohol. When drunk, they could have murdered the captain and his family. Later, they could have escaped using a lifeboat, which might have sunk in heavy seas. The sailors would have found a cargo of alcohol very tempting when alone at sea.

Theory Two
Aliens might have abducted the captain and his crew. There was no sign of a struggle aboard ship, so the aliens could have put them all in a trance. Nobody knows the reason for aliens abducting people, if, indeed, aliens exist. They may have wanted to experiment with the humans back on their own planet.

Theory Three
The ship was carrying raw alcohol. Raw alcohol can become unstable. Raw alcohol is, therefore, dangerous and can explode. The captain and his crew might have been worried about a possible explosion and he might have launched a lifeboat (one was missing). The lifeboat could have sunk in heavy seas.

Theory Four
The sailors might have disliked Captain Briggs. There could have been a mutiny on board. The sailors would then have murdered the captain and his family. They would have thrown the bodies overboard and escaped by lifeboat.

Theory Five
Pirates may have taken control of the ship and murdered those on board. They may have left the ship empty, because they were worried that the alcohol would explode.

Theory Six
A sea-monster might have snatched the crew and taken them under water. It would have eaten them in its secret lair. The ocean is so deep that there might be sea monsters hidden at the bottom of the ocean. They could surface every now and then, to eat whatever they can find.

Having worked through this mystery, students might like reading a further mystery and writing their own possible answers to it. The groups can then debate which solution appears the most likely. Here is one idea students can use, which is also available online:

Crop circle mysteries
Crop circles are unexplained designs that appear in crops during the night. Crop circles appear all over the world in simple forms but they appear in Britain more than anywhere else in the world!

Crop circles are found mostly in fields of corn, oat, grass and rice. They have sometimes appeared in sand or snow. Additionally, they have appeared around ancient sites, such as Stonehenge.

Where crop circles appear, the plants seem to change. They look dehydrated.

The crops often have interesting patterns. The plants swirl in a clockwise or anti-clockwise direction. Sometimes the stalks look woven. Occasionally, when aircraft have flown over the crop circles, their compasses have spun out of control. Watches and mobile phones have not worked correctly and cameras have failed to work.

Crop circles have appeared inside restricted areas, such as military land in Wiltshire, which is fenced off.

Some people who have visited crop circles have felt sick and suffered headaches or dizziness. After leaving the crop sites, some people have actually been physically sick.

There are many theories about crop circles. Can you think of any?

After these two exercises, the students should be able to research and write about a mystery that appeals to them. If stuck, they should research the Yeti or Bigfoot.

Drama as a learning tool
Monologues
Students usually enjoy writing and performing their own monologues. They also enjoy positively marking the performance of others. This activity will give you a chance to assess their writing skills, and their speaking and listening skills. It is also available online.

Computer Nerd
I can zap twenty aliens in one go –
I'm brave. I dodge the bullets and destroy the enemy base.
At the press of a button, I can enter a dungeon and answer questions from the ugly dungeon master.
My sword raised, I can hack my way through the many headed monsters and find the golden key that will unlock the correct door.

I have completed many quests.
I have attended King Arthur's court and drunk mead with the great king.
I killed the Red Knight who'd imprisoned the maiden with golden hair.

I can play football for any team. I scored the crucial goal in the fantasy FA Cup Final.
I took Bolton to the top of the Premiership and I won the World Cup for Canada!

I can design the biggest theme park in the world and I've watched happy customers slide down the highest helter-skelter anyone can build.

I have travelled to strange planets and fought in intergalactic wars.

I can do anything – as long as I have my computer switched on and my chair is comfortable.

I can conquer the world!

Why, if I can do all this, am I such a loner at school?
By Keith West (2005a, with permission from First and Best in Education)

Students can now look at the activities.

In pairs, read 'Computer Nerd' and then re-read the monologue. Before you perform the piece, think about the following points:

- Speak clearly and make sure you can be heard.
- Look at your audience; do not spend all the time looking down at your script.
- Decide on the best voice for each particular part in the monologue.
- Use the sound of words effectively. *Example:* 'I *dodge* the bullets and *destroy* the enemy base. You could place an emphasis on the 'd' words, which are both verbs.
- Vary your tone and pitch to make the monologues more interesting.

As an extra activity, ask the students to decide what they think the monologue is about. They should point out that the computer nerd is a hero in cyber world. In the real world, he is a lonely person. The students can now answer the following questions:

- What adjective is used to describe the dungeon master? Can you think of more effective adjectives to describe him?
- Do you think the computer nerd is a boy or a girl? Give reasons for your answer.
- What six different games does the computer nerd play?

For additional work, look at the following suggestions:

1. Imagine that 'Computer Nerd' is to be made into a film. Write a storyboard for the film.

Casting, for the film: Imagine famous people are to star in the film 'Computer Nerd'. Next to the cast list, suggest a famous person who might fit the bill. The people chosen might be famous filmstars, sports personalities or politicians. This is also available online.

Cast list
The computer nerd
Helpless blond maiden
An assassin

Goalkeeper
Dungeon master
Footballer
Many-headed monster
Pilot
King Arthur
Alien One
Alien Two
The Red Knight

2. Hot-seating
   In small groups, hot-seat the computer nerd and ask him/her questions, such as why are computer games so addictive?

3. A play version of 'Computer Nerd'
   Students would enjoy turning the monologue into a play. They can use the information from their storyboard to write the play.

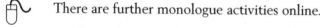 There are further monologue activities online.

Duologues

This activity allows students to perform. I believe that students who are not confident with their reading, are able to handle small parts in a play. Sometimes, though, they miss their part and the class becomes bored. Duologues allow students to read short extracts but, as there are only two readers, they are able to keep on task. If they go on to write their own duologues, either in pairs or individually, they are also fulfilling a writing task.

Tell the students that this is an activity which requires working in pairs. Then ask them to read through the duologue, practise it and read it out loud.

In this activity, it is best to go around the groups and listen to some of the pairs perform. If there is a particularly good pair performance, you could stop the class and allow the pair to model their performance to the rest of the group. They then know the standard they need to attain. This script is also available online in case you would like to hand it out to the students.

Yo Yo Kid

Yo Yo Kid meets a friend he has not seen for some time. They get talking . . .

(We do not know the names of Yo Yo Kid or the friend, so the duologue can be performed by either sex.)

Friend (*concerned*): You seem a bit down lately.

Yo Yo (*depressed*): Yeah, I'm a kid of this generation. I'm twenty-first century kid. I'm one of the many yo yo kids.

Friend: Yo yo kid? What's a yo yo kid?

Yo Yo: I'll tell you. A yo yo kid is someone whose parents are divorced.

Friend (*thinking*): Yeah, I remember now, yours split up a few months back, didn't they? Hasn't your mum found a new fella?

Yo Yo (*tetchy*): That's the whole point. I'm, like, homeless. Some days, the days of the week, I'm at mum's house and she nags me about homework and school and that . . . and when step-dad comes home they get all huddled up together and I know I'm not wanted.

Friend (*sympathetic*): It's like that at home for me, too, sometimes. Then I go up to my bedroom and listen to my music – with the earphones on. I mustn't disturb mum and dad . . . they run a business and need time to plan.

Yo Yo: My mum and step-dad cuddle up on the settee and share their little secrets together.

Friend: But why do you call yourself Yo Yo Kid?

Yo Yo (*upset*): Well, Friday night and most weekends I'm with dad. He drives me to the old house, our old house . . . when we were a family. It's dirty now; there are coffee stains on the carpet.

Friend (*confused*): Your dad – he's friendly and cheerful isn't he? Least, that's how I remember him.

Yo Yo: Yeah, and he takes me to the Saturday matches. He tells me I'm great. He tells me stories of when he was a kid.

Friend (*more confused*): So why don't you go and live with him?

Yo Yo: He wouldn't want me with him all the time. He'd rather be with his mates. That's why I'm a yo yo kid . . . I belong to two homes but I don't really belong to any.

(West, 2005b, with permission from First and Best in Education)

Use this as an activity sheet for the students.

In pairs take turns to be the Yo Yo Kid and his/her friend. Tell the students to think about the following points before they perform the duologue:

- Speak clearly and make sure you can be heard.
- Look at your audience – do not spend time looking down at your script.
- Make sure you come in on time.
- Show a reaction to what the other person is saying. Use expressions and hand gestures when appropriate.
- Vary your tone and pitch to make the duologue more interesting.

Should you wish to use additional activities, following are some suggestions:

Tell the students to improvise a scene between Yo Yo Kid and his/her mum and step-dad. The Yo Yo Kid could be telling them what he/she has already told the friend. What might the mum and step-dad's reaction to the Yo Yo Kid be?

Ask the students to stay in pairs and write their own duologue on one of the following themes:

- A person is telling a friend about winning the lottery. The friend tries to persuade the winner to share the wealth.
- A person is telling somebody that there has been a robbery. The other person knows who the robber might be.
- A child wants a puppy for Christmas but a parent tries to persuade the child that a puppy is not a good idea. Both the child and the parent need to state and defend their reasons.

 There is a short duologue extra online.

Both the monologue and the duologue are appropriate for KS3 classes. It is possible to present monologues to KS4 classes as either an introduction to Shakespeare or as an introduction to a particular play. I have also used these monologues as revision pieces.

Romeo and Juliet

If the students are about to study *Romeo and Juliet* or need to revise the play, try the following monologue. It is also available online.

Juliet's Lament

I should have married the County Paris. That's what my parents wanted and my nurse eventually advised me to do. Instead, like a fool I was, I married my families' enemy. I fell in love with the dangerous one, the one who lived on the edge.

Romeo was a man of emotions and impulses, a man willing to destroy himself rather than lose my love.

A woman will never love the safe one, the right one, the steady one, the one who can offer security and comfort. She will always find a fatal attraction in the one she shouldn't touch. She's done this since Eve disobeyed God and followed the snake into the orchard and stood beneath the tree of the fruit that offered all knowledge. As she bit into the fruit that looked so desirable, she knew the difference between good and evil. She lost her innocence and I fell backwards for my Romeo, but I had no wit or wisdom, only the fatal flaw – the temptations of Eve.

My only love sprang from my only hate.

My problem was that I loved my cousin's loathed enemy. I was forced to marry in secret, my parents would never agree to such a union as ours.

And then, before our marriage was consummated, my one love had killed my cousin Tybalt. Did Romeo's hand shed Tybalt's blood? Did ever dragon keep so fair a cave? (pause) But I must support my husband! I cannot blame him, if he had not killed Tybalt, then Tybalt would have slain him.

And we had that brief glimpse of happiness before Romeo was banished. He, my husband, slept in my bed while my parents, innocent of Romeo's presence, arranged a marriage with County Paris.

How could I pretend I had never married Romeo, as my traitor nurse suggested? Oh, yes, the Friar would have his reasons to keep quiet . . . he had married us in secret and against the wishes of our parents.

Yes, I could have married Paris and nobody would have believed a banished murderer. But I had to keep loyal to my true husband, Romeo.

The Friar's desperate plan might have worked out. I **did** drink his potion, I **did** pretend to die. I **was** buried in the family vault alongside my dead cousin, Tybalt.

All was going to plan!

Curse the Friar for not ensuring his letter reached my Romeo. Romeo thought I really was dead and he came to find my dead body. Romeo, a man of impulses, drank deadly poison and fell down beside me.

What? Are thy lips still warm, my Romeo?

Then I must die. I cannot live without you.

Ah, Romeo still has his dagger.

(Juliet picks up the dagger.)

I cannot go with the cowardly Friar to a nunnery, to live my life with regrets and live through long tedious days. Nothing will ever be the same without my man of danger, without the one who lives on the edge. I shall die!

(She thrusts the dagger into her body.)

Romeo!

(Juliet falls down dead.)

(West 2005c, with permission from First and Best in Education)

If monologue was a revision exercise, the students can look at the following activities.

Discussion

- What ideas are mentioned in the monologue that do not appear in the play?
- In the monologue Juliet compares herself (and women in general) with Eve. Do you think the merging of Biblical events into a Shakespeare play works? Give reasons for your answers.

Hot-seating characters from *Romeo and Juliet*

- Hot-seat characters from the play and ask them to answer in role. Invent two questions each, to ask a particular character. *For example:*

To Prince Escalus: Why did you not punish offenders of the first public brawl with greater severity?

Writing

- Write an essay entitled, Who or what is responsible for the deaths of Romeo and Juliet?

Think of all the characters and things that might be responsible for the death of the two lovers in some way. You may wish to include the following:

- Prince Escalus;
- Paris;
- Tybalt;
- Capulet;
- Friar Lawrence;
- The Apothecary;
- Benvolio;
- Mercutio;
- Juliet's nurse;
- Romeo and Juliet themselves;
- Fate (star-crossed lovers).

Looking at the characters, what do we know about the following (also available online)?

Character	Good points	Bad points
Romeo	A courteous gentleman	Impulsive
Tybalt		
Mercutio		
Juliet		
The Nurse		
The Friar		

As an additional revision exercise, ask the class to make a monologue of their own, finding evidence from the play and using Mercutio, Tybalt, Benvolio or the Friar as their characters.

Macbeth

Perhaps you are studying *Macbeth* with your class. The character of Macbeth can also make a good monologue, this is also available online.

Macbeth's Lament

What was that burning ambition that led to my destruction? Those witches knew what they were doing, meeting me on the heath. They knew I was consumed by envy, greed and the desire to attain greatness, whatever the cost. They knew I wanted all from the very flowering of my youth. They knew all this when they met me on the heath.

Why did I unseam the enemy from the nave to the chaps? Why did I fix the enemy's head upon the royal battlements? Not because I loved old Duncan, a good king but too old and frail to join the battle. No, I did not risk my life for the common good but I risked all because I loved myself. I wanted further advancement. I wanted people to see me as brave and valiant. The witches knew I would fall pray to their evil powers.

The Witches! Their limited evil powers gave them foreknowledge, told them I would become the next Thane of Cawdor – so they teased me and greeted me as the future king. They told me a truth to win me to their harm, to make sure I would be forever damned.

Why did I write to my wife and tell her all the witches told me? My foolish, ambitious wife whom I once loved. I wish I'd kept the witches' prophesy to myself. Lady Macbeth knew I wanted the golden crown but she knew I would not bend to evil, unless persuaded.

And so, I killed the much loved Duncan and allowed his children to flee into exile. I gained the crown and became the king of Scotland. I could now live my dreams. But there were always whispers; and Banquo, my great and best friend since the days of my youth, knew the truth. He had to die, too. The witches had given me a barren crown. Did they not tell Banquo that his children would rule at some stage after my death? I had to kill him and his son, I had to defy fate.

My greatest friend, the loyal Banquo, was dispatched. But Fleance, his son, escaped. I knew that one day he was destined to rule.

What is this ambition? It is nothing more than the bitter taste of dust. What did I gain from murdering Duncan? I lost my best friend when he died. I lost my wife's love and her sanity. I hardened my heart and committed foul deeds such as the butchering of Macduff's wife and children. I lost my dignity and my self-respect. All my subjects came to fear and hate me. I became a cancer on the face of Scotland.

I was isolated. Men obeyed me out of fear rather than love. I became a hell hound whom all despised.

Now is the time that I must pay for my crimes. Hell opens up before me and it is murky, dark and full of horrors.

(West, 2005d, with permission from First and Best in Education)

I have given students this monologue as a revision piece after they have studied the text. KS5 students have also used this monologue as a performance piece for their drama work. Some students have also used it as exemplar work to show lecturers before applying for drama college.

If you wish to use it as a revision piece, follow-up activities could be:

Discussion

- Do you think this interpretation is correct? Would Macbeth be thinking these things or is some of the monologue incorrect? If you think parts of the monologue are incorrect, find evidence in the text to support your views.
- Re-read the monologue and list Macbeth's regrets.

Writing

If you know the play well, write a monologue from the point of view of Macduff. You might wish to mention:

- His suspicions about Macbeth's involvement in Duncan's murder.
- Reflecting on his wife's point of view.
- His thoughts on hearing about the murder of his wife and children.
- His desire for revenge.
- His final meeting with Macbeth.

Soliloquies

Have a look at Lady Macbeth's soliloquy (Act 1: Scene 5). She is reading a letter from Macbeth and she is reflecting on his character. This is also available online.

Lady Macbeth's soliloquy

They met me on the day of success, and I have learn'd by the perfect'st report they have more in them than mortal knowledge. When I burn'd in desire to question them further, they made themselves air, into which they vanish'd. Whiles I stood rapt in the wonder of it, came missives from the King, who al-hail'd me 'Thane of Cawdor,' by which title, before, these weird sisters saluted me, and referr'd me to the coming on of time, with 'Hail, King that shalt be!' This have I thought good to deliver thee, my dearest partner of greatness, that though mightst not lose the dues of rejoysing by being ignorant of what greatness is promis'd thee. Lay it to thy heart, and farewell.

Glamis thou art, and Cawdor; and shalt be what thou art promis'd. Yet do I fear they nature;
It is too full o'th' milk of human kindness
To catch the nearest way. Thou wouldst be great:
Art not without ambition, but without
The illness should attend it. What thou wouldst highly,
That wouldst thou holily: wouldst not play false,
And yet wouldst wrongly win,
Thou'dst have, great Glamis, that which cries
"Thus thou must do" if thou have it;

And that which rather thou doest fear to do
Than wishest should be undone. Hie thee hither,
That I may pour my spirits in thine ear,
And chastise with the valour of my tongue
All that impedes thee from the golden round.
Which fate and metaphysical aid doth seem
To have thee crown'd withal.
(Enter a messenger.)
What is your tidings?
(Lady Macbeth hears that the king will be lodging at Macbeth's castle that night. She continues her soliloquy.)
Come, you spirits
That tend on mortal thoughts, unsex me here;
And fill me, from the crown to the toe,
Top-full
Of direst cruelty. Make thick my blood,
Stop up th'access and passage to remorse,
Shake my fell purpose nor keep peace between
Th' effect and it. Come to my woman's breasts,
And take my milk for gall, you murd'ring ministers,
Wherever your sightless substances
You wait on nature's mischief. Come, thick night,
And pall thee in the dunnest smoke of hell,
That my keen knife see not the wound it makes,
Nor heaven peep through the blanket of the dark
To cry 'Hold, hold'.

Then ask the students the following questions:

- Macbeth 'burns' in desire to question the witches further. What does this tell us about his character?
- How do we know the witches are not mortal?
- What truthful statements have the witches told Macbeth?
- How do these truths lead Macbeth into harm?
- Why does Macbeth tell his wife exactly what happened on the heath?
- How does Macbeth change towards his wife after he becomes king?
- What are Lady Macbeth's worries about her husband in Act 1: Scene 5?
- What does she mean by 'catch the nearest way'?
- How does Lady Macbeth intend to persuade Macbeth to kill Duncan in Act 1: Scene 5?
- How does Lady Macbeth intend to change and what happens to her later to suggest the change was only for a short period of time?

Other activities for *Macbeth*

Thinking about Banquo

Ask the students the following question: Many people who study the play believe that Banquo is a good character, but is he? For example, why did he not tell Duncan about the witches? Did he forget, or was he ambitious for his children?

Allow the students to discuss the question and work out what they believe Banquo's character is really like.

Drama

In groups, students take on a character from the play and defend their position. Ask them to explain why they acted as they did and try to prove that they could not have acted in any other way.

Soliloquies

In small groups, try practising a soliloquy. Use either Lady Macbeth's speech (Act 1: Scene 4) starting after she enters the play, reading the letter or Macbeth's speech (Act 1: Scene 7) starting 'If it were done when 'tis done'.

Think about:

- pace;
- time;
- emphasis;
- delivery.

Macbeth's speech, Act 1: Scene 7

If it were done when 'tis done,
then 'twere well.
It were done quickly. If th' assassination
could trammel up the consequence, and catch,
with his surcease, success; that but this blow
Might be the be-all and the end-all here –
But here upon this bank and shoal of time-
We'd jump the life to come. But in these cases
We still have judgement here, that we but teach
Bloody instructions, which being taught
Return
To plague th' inventor. This even-handed
Justice
Commends th' ingredience of our poison'd
Chalice
To our own lips. He's here in double-trust:
First, as I am his kinsman and his subject-
Strong both against the deed; then, as his host,
Who should against his murderer shut the door,

Not bear the knife myself. Besides, this Duncan
Hath borne his faculties so meek, hath been
So clear in his great office, that his virtes
Will plead like angels, trumpet-tongu'd, against
The deep damnation of his taking-off;
And pity, like a naked new-born babe,
Striding the blast, or heaven's cherubin
Hors'd
Upon the sightless couriers of the air.
Shall blow the horrid deed in every eye,
That tears shall drown the wind. I have
No spur
To prick the sides of my intent, but only
Vaulting ambition, which o'er-leaps itself,
And falls on th'other.

By William Shakespeare (1951)

This extract is also available online.

Once the students have read the above speech, ask them the following questions:

- What is Macbeth's first concern about killing Duncan?
- What is Macbeth's second concern? What does he mean by a 'poison'd chalice'?
- What sort of king does Macbeth feel Duncan has become? Does he think Duncan is a good or bad king?
- What is Macbeth's only reason for killing Duncan?
- How does Macbeth's thoughts on Duncan's kingship contrast with Macduff's desire to kill Macbeth later in the play?

Essay writing

Ask the students to choose one of the following:

- How does Lady Macbeth persuade Macbeth to kill Duncan?
- Discuss the role of evil in the killing of Duncan.
- Discuss the role of women in the play.

Working with KS4 students, there may be an opportunity to ask them to write a dramatic monologue as a piece of coursework. When they perform the monologue, it can be used as a speaking and listening activity. Students enjoy writing monologues and if the monologue can be assessed for two different reasons, that can only be a bonus . . . and an incentive for students to write at their highest potential.

'Sinister Monologue' (below) was performed by a Year 10 student I taught a few years ago. Do use it as an example of what can be achieved by an average student. This is also available online.

Sinister Monologue

(party music)

Bye everyone. I've had a great time. I enjoyed the food, the wine and the music. Now I've got to go home. What? No, I can't stay longer. No, I really do have to go. I'll be fine. I can't wait for the others. Mum made me promise I'd be home before midnight. Thanks for everything. The party was really great. See you all on Monday. Yes, I'll take the short cut through the woods.

(Cheryl starts walking)

I'm glad to be away from that loony bunch. What a rotten choice in music. Who likes 'Folk' these days? The food they had the cheek to serve up made me feel sick! I didn't like the look of that fat boy with the greasy hair. All he did was stare at me. Who was he anyway? Never seen him before! He gave me the creeps. He sat in the corner of the room all evening and stared at me. He didn't even say hello.

(Cheryl enters the woods, an owl hoots)

This is the only part of the walk I don't like. The woods. I shall soon be home . . . tucked up in my cosy warm bed. The woods are creepy, they cast eerie shadows . . . and the moon isn't out, there are too many clouds covering the sky. Where are the stars? I'm cold. There are the wild woods, like that play we did in Year 7, 'Toad of Toad Hall'. Evil lurks in the woods, I can feel evil. I have a strange feeling . . . somebody is following me.

(There is the definite sound of footsteps)

There! I **can** hear footsteps. Don't panic, keep calm. When I walk, I hear footsteps. When I stop, I hear nothing. My friends, I wish you were all here with me. If I run . . . the footsteps increase, they're gaining on me. I'll pretend I'm with somebody.

(Cheryl pretends she is with friends)

'Did you hear that, Becky?'
'Yes, **good job** my boyfriend's going to meet us.'
'Can you see him, Cheryl?'
'Yes, Lizzie . . . let's run and meet him.'
'Great idea, Tracy. We'll **all** run and meet him. Then we can tell him about the nasty person who's following us!'
I wonder if that'll work. Right. I'd better run now!

(Cheryl runs, screams, falls and picks herself up, dejected)

I must wash my hands. I must be clean. No soap will wash away this . . . this defilement. That fat greasy haired man . . . was his name Vince? . . . only got a few years. I have a life sentence. No, I dare not go outside – not even to the shops – not alone. I am imprisoned inside my own home. I must wash my hands. My hands. They are so cracked, so sore. Look at my hands! *(shouts at*

audience) If only I could clean them . . . wash away that night . . . the image
of that man.
(West 2005e, with permission from First and Best in Education)

For group discussion exercises with this monologue, try the following
questions with the students. They can either work individually or in
pairs:

- Looking at the first 13 lines, what are the differences between
  what Cheryl says as she leaves the party and what she is really
  thinking?
- At what point does the mood and atmosphere first change?
- How would you evoke mood and atmosphere? Would you
  create mood by playing background music at various points,
  for example? If so, when?
- Cheryl has obviously been through an horrific experience.
  How would you council her to regain confidence?
- What punishment do you feel is appropriate for Vince?
- How can Vince be counselled so that he can feel responsible
  for what he has done?
- How can Cheryl be counselled so that she can live a normal
  life again? What advice would you give Cheryl if you were her
  best friend?
- How would you suggest the part of Cheryl is played? The role
  requires a wide range of voice and movement to sustain and
  develop the dramatic action. The actress needs four different
  voices for the part in the action when she pretends she is with
  her friends. Discuss when you would change the tone and the
  range of voice. What movements would you make and when?
  For example, the final few lines may require the actress to kneel
  on the floor, washing her hands using a rhythmic motion.

Extended activities
Improvisation

- Imagine that Cheryl has just left the party. Two of her friends
  talk about her. Act out a discussion between the two friends.
  They discuss her attitude towards them and the party. They
  talk about her stated reasons for leaving the party but do they
  understand her real reasons? Are they able to read between
  the lines?
- The same friends meet the following day, having learned of
  Cheryl's experience. They have a further discussion. Will
  their attitude towards Cheryl have changed in light of what
  happened to her? Are they sympathetic or do they feel she

made a decision to leave the party early, so she can only blame herself for what happened?

Writing

- As Lizzie (or Damien), write a letter to an older brother (or sister) telling him/her all about the party and what happened afterwards.

Using hot-seating to reinforce learning

Hot-seating is useful to allow students to question characters 'in role'. It is a good revision tool at GCSE. For example, taking the play 'An Inspector Calls' (Priestly, 1946), a student can volunteer to play Mr Birling and the rest of the group can then ask Mr Birling questions. The questions need to be relevant to the text.

'Mr Birling, what is your favourite meal at breakfast time?' is not a good question because there is no evidence from the text to show what Mr Birling prefers to eat for breakfast. Students need to be reminded that questions need to be relevant to the text.

'Mr Birling, what is your attitude towards your son?' is a relevant question, as there is plenty of evidence in the text to show what Mr Birling's attitude towards his son is – through his words and actions and also through Eric's words and actions.

This kind of activity will show you, as a teacher, how much individual students know about the text. You will quickly discover what you need to do or what individual students need to do, to ensure that the class knows the text and is prepared for the exams.

Freeze-framing

In this activity, students can take a moment in a text and build up a picture-image of what is happening. Take *To Kill a Mocking Bird* (Lee, 1960) – students might choose to freeze-frame the moment Atticus shoots Tim Johnson (the dog with rabies). They will need to work out who else is in the action at that particular moment, so they will need to study that part of the text very carefully. You can ask them why that particular incident is important to the story as a whole. You should get the answer that it shows the reader that Atticus is brave – he is willing to stand in the street and face a dog with rabies. You might also get that it prepares the reader for the court scene, when Atticus stands alone to defend Tom Robinson. A really fine answer would be that it changes Jem's attitude towards his father, when he learns that Atticus was known as 'one-shot Finch'. A useful revision exercise!

If students are working on their own creative scripts, you can ask them to freeze-frame an important moment in them. They have to explain why that particular moment is important to the story as a whole. This exercise ensures that the students are working hard on their scripts or improvised pieces at all times. They have to keep on task because they never know when you are going to freeze-frame the action!

Once the action is frozen, the group has to immediately tell you what is happening in the drama and how the piece of drama will develop further.

Creating a thought tunnel is another possible revision exercise. Students create a tunnel by forming two parallel lines and touching finger tips with the person opposite. A volunteer then walks through the tunnel as a character. Take George from *Of Mice and Men*. As 'George' walks through the tunnel, the group whispers what he might be thinking at any point in the novel. 'George' walks slowly through the tunnel and each member of the tunnel needs to say something.

You might have students say the following:

- 'Why am I lumbered with Lennie?'
- 'I think Slim listens to me.'
- 'Curley's wife is dangerous.'
- 'I hope Lennie stays well away from Curley.'
- 'I'll allow Lennie to tend the rabbits.'
- 'I know I have to shoot Lennie. He's my responsibility.'

This activity should reinforce what the students already know and can form part of a revision exercise.

Giving witness

In small groups, the students can set up a court. They can imagine a character is on trial. Take Friar Lawrence from *Romeo and Juliet*. He could face trial for his involvement in the deaths of Romeo and Juliet. In this exercise, you will need a judge, a defending lawyer, the prosecution and Friar Lawrence. Students can be divided into groups of four. They may ask the following questions:

- 'Why did you allow Romeo and Juliet to marry in secret?'
- 'Why did you devise a plan to pretend Juliet was dead?'
- 'Why didn't you take the important letter to Romeo yourself?'
- 'Why did you run away from the Capulet tomb and leave Juliet alone with the dagger?'

All the above questions are relevant and the answers can be found in the text.

This exercise can form part of a speaking and listening activity and can be fun in that the defending lawyer can interrupt with relevant issues and ask his own questions, to aid the friar:

- 'Is it true that you allowed Romeo and Juliet to marry in order that the family feud might end?'

If performed correctly, this is a good revision exercise.

Re-enactments

This exercise is another way of reinforcing drama texts. Students can re-enact a scene from *Macbeth* and stop at a certain point in order that the class can look at its dynamics and tensions. The discussion between Macbeth and Lady Macbeth, that leads up to the death of Duncan, is a good scene to re-enact (Act 1: Scene 7).

This activity allows students to fully comprehend what is happening at a particular part of a text.

The dinner party

Write out the names of each character the students are studying for literature at GCSE. Write each name on a separate piece of paper. For example, a class might be studying *Macbeth* and *Of Mice and Men* for their GCSE texts.

Give each student a piece of paper with a name on that paper. The class then splits into groups of six. Each student then looks at his/her paper. The student then joins the other five members of the group for a 'dinner party'.

During this piece of improvisation, each student has to keep in character. To distinguish male from female characters, you may need to use blue and pink paper. In the example given, some girls will need to take on male roles.

For example, at the party there may be Macbeth, Lady Macbeth, Curley's wife, Slim, Carlson and Banquo. They will need to talk. They could discuss their role in the play/novel or they may talk about other things. It is essential that they act in character. If students can keep in character, it will prove that they have understood the essentials of a text.

Your role is to listen to the groups as they talk. You could allow one group to share its dinner party with the other groups. Choose a group that appears to be doing well!

The detective

In pairs, allow the students to become the detective and the witness or suspect. I have allowed classes to play this game when studying *Macbeth*. A 'detective' could interview Macbeth concerning the suspicious death of King Duncan. Or Lady Macbeth could be interviewed concerning the very suspicious murder of Banquo.

This exercise is useful for reinforcing the understanding of a text. You might find the following:

Detective: I believe you discovered Duncan's body?

Macbeth: No, Macduff discovered the murdered king in his chamber.

(It might be that the detective is asking a trick question or, more likely, that the student forgot/did not realize Macduff discovered the king was murdered. The student playing Macbeth puts the 'detective' right, so a learning situation has taken place, which you can reinforce.)

Another possible lead in could be:

Detective: I'm suspicious that Duncan was murdered in your castle . . . and you have the most to gain.

Macbeth: I was set up by Duncan's sons but they lacked courage and fled.

(Macbeth's answer is very good here and it appears that the student knows the text very well.)

This is a good activity for students who have read and studied the text once. The exercise allows you to discover if they have understood the text.

From book to script

I have always found that students enjoy turning an exciting part of a book into a script. You can either find a short story or the class reader and ask them to turn part of the story into a script. When completed, the students can act it out. To keep the students on task, or give them a competitive edge, the audience can mark for content, acting ability and vocabulary. This gives members of the audience something positive to focus on while they wait their turn to perform. They then have to justify their marks, which will keep them alert.

Before writing, students need to be reminded of the following:

- When scriptwriting, the character's name appears on the left-hand side of the page. If the script is typed, the name needs to be in bold.
- There is a colon after the character's name.
- What the character actually says goes after the colon.
- Stage directions are written in italics and are surrounded by brackets.

Taking an exciting part of a class reader and turning it into a script reinforces the students' understanding of the novel in an interesting way. If they are able to keep the characters' behaviour and speech 'in character' they will quickly realize the author's craft.

Following is the beginning of a story. Ask the students to read the story through in small groups. When they understand the story, ask them to turn it into a script. They can do this in their groups or individually. If they work on their own then they need to come together and decide which of the group has written the best script to act out. This extract is also available online.

The dumb game

I'll tell you from the start, I didn't want to nick anything. The others were determined. I didn't want to loose cred in their eyes. I wanted to be a part of them, of their gang. I wanted to do what they did. I wanted to belong. Crazy? Yes, sure. But I was fed up of being on the outside.

We sauntered into this big department store. Simon's eyes wandered over the store like he'd done this sort of thing a thousand times before. A professional, I thought.

'No cameras,' he hissed.

Jolene touched my nervous shoulder. 'So you wanna be in our gang, Meacher,' she said. She smiled but her smile was not kind. Her whole being was like poison. I didn't like the way she called me Meacher rather than Jake. I shrugged my shoulders, pretending I didn't care. But I cared, cared too much.

'You nick something good and we'll get out fast,' said Josh in his casual, calm voice. In a voice that suggested normality. Yes, the gang stole. They'd probably done this every day of their rotten little lives.

I wandered over to the electrical goods. There was an attendant, a big man who looked as if he'd done a round or two with Mohammed Ali and come off the worse for wear.

Simon nudged me, 'Not here, Jake.' He led me to the record department. This store was daft enough to keep the CD's in their plastic jackets on full display.

'Pinch a CD and you're in . . . one of us!' he said.

Jolene scowled and looked bored. 'Yeah, yeah, whatever. He hasn't the guts,' she said. She made me angry, she made me want to steal even the crown jewels. I'd do anything to prove her wrong. To shove the CD right up her piggy nose just to show her.

I looked round the store.

'We'll wait for you outside,' said Gareth. 'We'll buy you a coke.'

Jolene sniggered. Simon winked at the security guard who nodded. He was a big man with muscle and a belly like a whale. I wondered why Simon had winked at him. Perhaps he was trying hard to be the cool kid.

I wanted to scream. I watched the gang go through the sliding glass doors and out into the street. The four of them, disappearing from the store like a ragged army. I glanced down at the CDs and grabbed the first one my hand hovered over. I don't even know what the title was or who was the singer. I slipped it into my combat trouser pocket and lurched towards the glass doors. I wanted out, out as quickly as possible.

The alarms sounded and the large security guard moved towards me with surprising speed for a big man. I was too scared to run. It was like I was in one of those dreams when you know you need to move quickly but you can't. Big belly caught hold of my arm. The four gang members were nowhere in sight. They hadn't waited for me.

Suddenly it all came to me, like the replay of some horror movie or like a flash of inspiration in a maths lesson. They'd set me up! They'd wanted me to get caught. Simon's wink, Jolene's taunting, Gareth's calm voice. They knew I'd get caught. The security man was in with the plot.

The four of them were probably with the other gang members right now, laughing their heads off. I sank to the floor and sobbed.

To turn that piece of writing into a play, students may need to add more dialogue and some extra information. The storyline (plot) should be the same.

Following is a possible play version of the story. It is also available online.

The dumb game playscript

Gareth *(speaks in a casual voice)*: You know the gang rules. You have to have guts to join this outfit.

Jake *(upset)*: I'm not nicking anything.

Simon *(laughing)*: What do you think we're about, Jake? We're not going on some teddy bear's picnic you know.

Jake: Yeah, but . . .

Jolene *(interrupting)*: Are you one of us, Jake, or are you a wimp?

(The four gang members snigger. They play football with a tin can until they arrive outside a big department store. All the time they played football with the can, Jake was excluded. He is obviously the outsider.)

Gareth *(stops and stares at Jake)*: Here we are, this store'll do.

(The five youths walk into the store.)

Jolene *(touches Jake's shoulder)*: So you wanna be in the gang, Meacher? You wanna be one of us?

Ask the students if they think that the play is a good version of the story. Could the opening be improved in any way?

Now ask the students to complete the play, looking at the text and keeping the storyline the same.

From script to book

Just as rewarding and enjoyable is turning a playscript into a book. If there is an old playscript in the English stockroom, ask students to turn the first scene of a play into prose. They may use as much description as possible and they can update an old storyline if they wish.

You may use the play below as an example, which is also available online.

The unreal world

Scene 1

(Craig and Lucy find a soldier slumped against a large oak tree. Beside him is a dead witch and a bag full of gold coins.)

Craig *(to soldier)*: Are you alright sir? You both look rather . . . unwell.

Lucy *(to Craig)*: The witch looks sicker than the soldier. She looks . . . kinda dead!

Soldier *(coming to his senses)*: Don't go down the hole in that big oak tree, children. There is a huge dog down there with eyes as big as saucers.

Craig *(to Lucy)*: I'd be more concerned about the size of its teeth.

Lucy: Are they bite size?

Soldier *(to the children)*: The dog is guarding a great amount of money. You could become very rich or you could die. Look at my torn trousers and the blood dripping from my ankles.

Craig *(sympathetic)*: So, the horrible dog with eyes as big as saucers bit you?

Soldier *(weary)*: No, the witch bit me before I killed her!

Lucy: So, you are a murderer! We should call the police. You can't go around killing old ladies just because they bite you.

Soldier *(uses his sword to help him stand and hobbles away)*: Well, I must be going. *(looks at witch)* Get somebody to bury the old hag or she'll stink the place out in a few days.

(The soldier hobbles off)

Craig *(peers down the hole in the tree)*: I think we can slide down the large hole, Lucy.

Lucy: And then what? We'll land in a place where there's a dog with large eyes.

Craig *(shrugs shoulders)*: In for a penny in for a pound. Our chance to get rich.

(Craig slides down the hole and lands in a large hall. Lucy follows him)

Witch *(rises from the ground)*: Ha, they all think me dead. I'll wait until those kids arrive back with the gold and then I'm made!

(Back in the hall Craig and Lucy look around)

Craig: I see no dog!

Lucy: No dog, but there's a massive wolf coming our way and it's dressed as a grandma.

Wolf *(looking very sly)*: Have you seen a little girl dressed in a red coat?

Lucy: With a red hood?

Wolf *(putting on a grandma type voice)*: Yes, yes! She's my poor little defenceless granddaughter.

Lucy: Well, I expect she'll be in the woods making her way over to your house.

Wolf *(slaps his forehead)*: Oh how stupid of me, I'm a silly wol . . . er – grandma. *(licks his lips)* Thanks nice, tasty, juicy children. *(to himself)* Think I'll stick around for a while. They might make a tasty meal.

A possible story from that script might be:

The unreal world script

On a bright and sunny evening, Craig and Lucy decide to take the short-cut home. Although the ancient woodland is rumoured to be a strange place where unexpected things happen, they still took the short-cut. They were late for tea and their mother has a temper when tea is spoiled.

The children follow a narrow path that will lead them to their village. All appears well until they spy a soldier slumped against an enormous old oak tree. Beside him is a witch. She looks like she's dead and there are flies buzzing around her ugly head.

Craig and Lucy could tell the old hag was a witch because she was wearing a witch's hat and black cloak. Her ugly face was pale and her eyes were open. She did not blink. She looked very dead. The soldier did not look the picture of health either.

Craig ran up to the soldier and asked him if he was alright. The injured soldier struggled up into a sitting position and grabbed hold of his long thin sword.

'Don't go down the hole in that oak tree kids. There is a huge dog with saliva dripping down its wobbly jaws. Its eyes are as big as saucers,' he said.

Craig looked at Lucy and she looked down at the injured soldier.

Ask the students if they think the start of story does justice to the play. Could the story be improved in any way?

Now ask the students to complete the story by reading the play and using information from it to write their story.

Remind them that plays are not descriptive, but stories can be. As the students are given the plot, through the play, they can then concentrate on describing the events surrounding the story. This activity should improve their ability to describe events.

Role play: somebody else's shoes (oral work)

This exercise is useful for Year 7 students. It allows them to gain empathy for characters in books. In this exercise, students need to gain empathy for other people who find themselves in a variety of situations.

Following are some examples for the students to work on:

1. Jason has left his homework on the school bus. He asks you if he can copy yours. What do you say?

   If your answer is yes, a week passes by. Your teacher points out that you and Jason have the same homework. One of you has copied! Before you can say anything, Jason tells the teacher that you have copied him. How do you feel?

   If your answer is no, Jason informs you that his dad is seriously ill in hospital. Jason was at the hospital all night. He still does not know if his dad will be alright. He lied about the homework being left on the bus because he didn't want anyone to know about his dad.

   If your answer is now 'yes' go to the first yes answer. If no, then Jason threatens to bully you. What do you do?

2. Improvise a situation when a new person has arrived in school. Some of you do not want anything to do with that person but others want to make friends. Discuss the situation in groups.
3. A tells B a secret that nobody should know about. B tells everyone A's secret. How do you think A will feel? How should A approach B now?

Book situations

1. Robert Knight has bunked off school to join older boys. They are SCWOC (stealing cars without owners' consent). They have stolen a car and then meet Robert. What does he do? Initially, he just wanted some fun. Does he withdraw from the situation or allow himself to get in deeper?
2. Mandy Edwick has discovered a large egg in her back garden. The egg rocks and it appears that something is about to hatch. Her friend, Jennie Mould, has told her that something flashed through the sky a few nights ago. It came from space. Jennie thought it was a spaceship about to crash but nobody has seen a crashed spacecraft. Is the egg something that came from space? What should Mandy do?
3. Carl Eastaway has seen a black van with no number plate. It's parked outside a bank. Suddenly, he hears gunshots and three men dash out of the bank. They are holding a girl hostage. They bundle her into the van and are about to drive away. What should Carl do?
4. There is a large explosion. Windows are blown out and there are screams. Leslie Fenlon sees that a large department store is on fire. She is sitting in a nearby cafe. She glances upwards. Through a smashed window she can see a young boy in a wheelchair. He is stuck on the second floor. There are flames and smoke. What does she do?

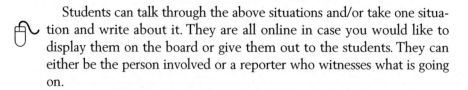

Students can talk through the above situations and/or take one situation and write about it. They are all online in case you would like to display them on the board or give them out to the students. They can either be the person involved or a reporter who witnesses what is going on.

Drama ideas bank (quick starters)

Following are further ideas to work through with the students.

Two of the students have to name everything to do with a particular category until one cannot think of any more in that category. They have 5 seconds to think of something. No repetitions allowed.

Example – Colours

(Students represented as A and B.)

A = Red

B = Blue

A = Yellow

B = Green

A = Brown

B = Violet

A = Black

B = Pink

A = White

B = ????

After 5 seconds of being unable to think of a colour, A wins! You can do this as a starter and as a warm up to other drama activities. This exercise can also be used as a finisher, to round off a lesson. I used to do this activity in form time or as a starter to a lesson, to allow students to think quickly. Colours is only an example, I've done this exercise asking students to think of vegetables, animals or famous people.

A story

I use this exercise at the start of a lesson, to get students thinking.

Start a story and ask somebody in the class to carry on. The title is very important – it has to be broad enough to allow lateral thinking. Students need to have the ability to broaden the story further – and if the story appears to be stagnating, take over and lead it in a new direction.

The rules are that everyone has to speak for a minute. After 1 minute, the student speaking needs to call out a name and the named person continues the story. Everyone in the class has one go. To make this exercise competitive, split the class into two teams. If a student 'dries up' and cannot speak for a minute, the team has lost a point. The team with the most points wins the game!

Possible title examples (all tried and tested):

- Alien invasion;
- The shapeshifter;
- The monster from the sea;
- Terror at school;
- The headteacher monster;
- Time traveller.

This exercise allows students to think quickly and, if done regularly, improves their imaginations.

Wink murder

This is a well-known game but if you have never played it, here are the rules.

This game is best done using somewhere with some space. Ask students to sit in a circle and close their eyes. Walk around the group and tap one student on the shoulder. That student becomes the detective and has to be in the centre of the circle. Tap another student twice on the shoulder. That student remains in the circle but is the murderer.

The object of the game is for the murderer to wink at as many people as possible before the detective catches the murderer. The detective is allowed three guesses.

To make the game really interesting, you can have two detectives. If you know the group, they can 'die' in an interesting way. For example, they can clutch their throats or twitch or scream as they are 'murdered'.

The small fish game

Ask the students to form a circle. They will need plenty of space. Go around the circle and name the 'fish'. The first is 'cod', the second is 'squid', the third is 'haddock' and the final fish is 'small fry'. The fifth is 'cod', the sixth is 'squid' and so on, until each member of the group is named. Shout out one of the fish names and all the 'fish' with that name need to run around the outside of the circle, clockwise. You step from the circle and into one of the spaces left by the named fish. The named fish then need to scramble for a space. One of the named fish will be out.

After a few rounds, place all of the group back into the circle, then name two fish groups. For example, 'Cod, run clockwise, small fry run anti-clockwise.' You can tell them that when you clap your hands, the fish need to change direction. Then, step into one of their spaces.

Continue to play until one group of fish has won.

The object of this exercise is for the class to let off steam before concentrating on specific drama work, such as looking at character.

Getting to know you

When you meet a new class the members of which do not know each other (typically Year 7 in their first week at secondary school), ask them to write down on a piece of paper five questions that they would like to know about other students, such as:

- What is your name?
- Do you have any brothers or sisters?
- Do you own a pet? If so what is it and what is its name?
- What's your favourite pop group?
- Where did you go on your last holiday?

Ask the students to walk around the room and then you shout 'stop'. Ask the students to talk to the nearest person that they do not know. They then take it in turns to ask the questions they have written down. Do this for about five turns then take one person from your group and ask the students, 'Who knows anything about this person?' Make sure that the students who answer your question have not known that person before. Hopefully, some of the students will remember some facts about that person!

This exercise is good for quickly bonding the group. A spin-off is that you get to know the names of a number of the students very quickly.

Balloon debates

In this piece of drama, allow students to work in groups of four or five. They need to imagine that they are a famous person – either living or dead. They need to individually research that person and know as much about that person as possible. 'Being' a famous person without knowing much about him/her makes for a dull balloon debate!

The balloon is sinking fast, all the ballast has been thrown out. Now somebody has to be sacrificed! Each student has to justify, in a short speech, why he/she needs to remain in the balloon. The class is given a vote and the student with the most votes wins. The student with the least votes is thrown out of the balloon.

Students can be – Lord Shaftesbury, England's best potential Football World Cup star, the Prime Minister, a British tennis player who is on his/her way to Wimbledon, a pop star about to perform at a concert.

Balloon debates can be used at GCSE level to reinforce the students' knowledge of a character.

Hot-air balloon literary version

Characters could be:

Mr Birling (from *An Inspector Calls*)
Eric Birling (from *An Inspector Calls*)
George (from *Of Mice and Men*)
Curley's wife (from *Of Mice and Men*)
Macduff (from *Macbeth*)
Lady Macbeth (from *Macbeth*)

From a practical point of view, give the students one lesson or a homework to research about a character and then place them in groups of four or five to perform. I would draw lots, to see which balloon is in the air first!

I prefer students sitting on chairs in front of the class and taking it in turns to give their speeches. I would then ask 'the floor' to think of a few questions for each candidate before taking a vote. If peer pressure or individual popularity are issues, I would then give each student a piece of paper and conduct a secret ballot.

Media – they've all watched a film

There is a number of exercises for English teaching purposes to do with the media. Most students know a great deal about films. Show them a clip of a film – or the first 5 minutes of one. Ask them to look at the technical codes – such as the camera angles. Then ask them to think through why the producer wanted the camera angles to be done in that particular way. Perhaps there was a shot of a person's face, looking tired and anxious. Or a shot of a whole person, rubbing her forehead, looking tired and anxious. Why did a producer decide on a particular shot or angle?

Then ask the students to think about the plot. Are there any clues in the plot to suggest what might happen next? How will the plot unfold? You can then show them more of the film, to allow the students to see if they have picked up any clues as to what would happen next.

Further suggested work to do with media

The students can think of an idea for a plot that they would like to turn into a film. If any student is stuck you could offer the following titles as a starting point:

- Trapped in space;
- Underwater adventure;
- The kidnapping;
- Horror mansion.

Students can thought-shower the plot and then storyboard the first scene.

For further work, the students can decide what famous actors might take on the characters in their film. Then, in pairs, students can take it in turns to interview a character from the film.

Example:
Interviewer: What made you decide you'd like the part of Stephen Blake in the film 'Horror mansion'?
Famous Actor: The part looked interesting. I've never played a baddie before, so it'll be a challenge.
Interviewer: So, can you tell me something about the plot?

(The students can continue the interview.)
Another possible exercise is to ask the students to design a poster advertising their film. This could be an interesting homework, allowing students to use their IT skills.

Students can then imagine that a pop band is writing songs for the film. They can make up a group name and describe the group members.

Example:

The Interrogators
Placid Sid – lead guitar. Far from placid, Sid writes most of the songs and is known for his temper tantrums on stage.
Lucky Wendy – also on guitar. She sometimes writes the softer ballads. Lucky is a misnomer, as her parents were killed in a freak accident when she was in her teens. She often hits the headlines for her wild lifestyle.

Students can then go on to write the songs for their group. The songs could be for a heavy metal group, for Hip/Hop, Rap or Country.

Having written a song or two for their group, students can design a pop festival poster featuring it.

Further media work could include:

- Television/radio – the pop interview.
- Popular music – the songs.
- Newspapers – all about the star of the film or the antics of a group member.
- Magazines – a review of the film.

Media studies in English at KS3 allows students an insight into media and an introduction to media studies as an informed understanding for a possible options choice for KS4. The work just done would be a relevant introduction into media studies.

There is an extra drama game online.

Use of circle time in English

Disruptive students can gain empathy for others through the use of circle time. Most students are familiar with circle time, used in one form or another.

I usually start circle time getting each student to say something about themselves. They often mention siblings, pets and their lives at home. They often mention sports they are involved in or sports they enjoy watching. I then allow them to talk about themselves for three revolutions around the circle.

I then challenge issues specific to that group or some individuals in that group. If some members of the group are disruptive at times, I then challenge their difficult behaviour. I might ask my students, 'Do you think it fair that some of you disrupt some lessons?' I never name individuals! 'Is it right and fair to stop others from learning?' 'Isn't it selfish?'

You may find that you discover some interesting reasons for

disruptive behaviour. For example, some students might find the work too difficult or they do not understand the work. In which case you make them a promise, 'I'll ask for a support teacher,' or 'I'll differentiate the work for you'.

You may also discover the following: 'He's better for you than for anyone else, Sir.' And 'You should see how he behaves in French.' That does not mean you then allow any disruption in your lesson, but you probe the reasons.

This exercise allows you to understand the students better and gives you the chance to put something in place to eradicate any form of disruption.

There needs to be firm ground rules for circle time. From the outset, allow students to understand that the circle is a circle of trust. Any talk within the circle is not for outside ears. They take turns to talk as the conversation passes around the circle. For some groups, you may physically need to pass around a beanbag. They can pass the beanbag on without speaking, but only the person holding the beanbag can speak.

A further value of circle time is that you, as an English teacher, are able to build up a good level of trust with your group. You get to know the group better; they get to know you better. The end product should be that the students are able to work as a team within your classroom. They see you as a human being! It's a win/win situation.

To work on circle time further, you will discover there are plenty of books to purchase on the subject. Resources exist with lesson plans.

As English is a subject that explores thoughts and feelings and requires empathy (as well as acquiring a body of knowledge), circle time is a very valuable exercise to undertake.

CHAPTER 7

Lessons that really work

Tribes

Literature at KS3: making the most out of Tribes

I have taught *Tribes* (Macphail, 2004) to a difficult mixed-ability Year 8 group, a further two Year 8 groups and two Year 9 groups. They all loved the book! In my opinion, every English stockroom should have it. This book is as successful as *Buddy*, by Nigel Hinton (1983).

The story starts with Kevin Davidson running and hiding from a gang. If caught, he would expect a beating. The excitement is intense and the students are immediately hooked! Kevin is saved by a rival gang, who are even more deadly.

After reading the first two chapters, students can research about gangs using the library or internet. Working in groups, they can present their information to the class.

The first two chapters give us some hints as to Kevin's character. Ask the students, 'What do we learn about Kevin's character at this point in the story?'

In Chapter 3 we are introduced to Kevin's family. Dad trusts Kevin and confides in him concerning his sister Glory. Ask the students, what do we learn about Kevin from this chapter? What do we learn about Salom – leader of 'The Tribe'? The students could write a few lines predicting what might happen next.

While reading Chapters 4 and 5, students enjoy predicting what they believe the initiation test might be. I ask them, at this point, to write down five possible initiation tests. They need to thought-shower the possibilities.

Students can make a chart of the main characters. Below is the start of one.

Character	Description	Evidence
Kevin	Sensible	'I'll keep an eye on her dad.'
Salom	Appears good but may not be	'Salom is Evil.'
Glory	Seems to know all the gossip	'Everyone's talking about it, Kev.'
Doc	Comes across as hostile.	'Doc doesn't like anybody.'

Students will be able to add to the chart as they read through the novel. By the end of the novel, they will have written down their thoughts concerning the main characters and they will have evidence to back-up their thoughts. They will be able to map how the characters develop and change as the novel progresses This is good training for GCSE work.

In Chapter 6 Kevin is introduced to the walk of death. The students could form a thought tunnel and whisper the thoughts Kevin would have as he is led blindfolded to the part of the building where the walk of death takes place. Students can whisper his thoughts as he realizes what he has to do.

From Chapter 7, I have 'performed' the walk of death reading the book and walking/wobbling over desk tops. I'm not suggesting that you follow my example. However, do read this chapter to the class and use pregnant pauses. Whisper Kevin's words, make them sound dramatic. The students do not know the outcome; they are not always too sure that Kevin will survive intact. You will find that you have a rapt and attentive audience. Their written work will reflect this!

For work on this chapter, tell the students to imagine a journalist has followed the group into the building. He is writing an article about the walk of death for the local newspaper. They are to be the journalist writing the article, as begun in the example below.

Crazy youths cheat death

A gang, known locally as The Tribe, has a dangerous initiation test that must be stopped.

Now ask the students to continue the article.

For further work, ask the students to write a diary entry from Kevin's point of view. He can write down his thoughts and feelings as he joins The Tribe. Has he any regrets or concerns?

In Chapter 8 readers learn about Stash. There is a hint that he dies trying the walk of death for a second time. Ask the students the questions, 'What does this tell us about The Tribe? Should Kevin have any concerns?'

Ask the students to bullet point how they think Kevin has changed in Chapter 9. They should think of his attitude towards Glory and Tommy. How has Kevin let Tommy down? How should you treat friends? Then ask the students why Kevin finds his friend less interesting than members of The Tribe.

Ask the students to bullet point how Kevin is further dragged into the ways of The Tribe in Chapter 10. They can develop their character track by adding to Kevin's profile and adding his mum and dad.

Ask the students, 'How do you think Tommy feels about Kevin joining The Tribe in Chapter 11?' As an exercise, the students can imagine that Tommy keeps a diary. He can write a few entries from before Kevin joins The Tribe until Tommy realizes his friendship with Kevin has changed. Tommy is loyal and he might feel that Kevin's loyalty is in question.

Imagine a TV crew has witnessed the incident in the shopping mall that occurs in Chapters 12 and 13. They are interviewing several people to discover what actually happened. They could interview Kevin's dad, Salom and Glory. In small groups, ask your class to conduct the interviews and present them to the rest of the class.

Students could bullet point ideas for revenge that Salom might have thought about in Chapter 14.

Ask the students what Chapters 15 and 16 tell us about Salom and Kevin. Should the secrecy concerning Stash make the reader feel uneasy about Salom?

I usually read Chapters 18, 19 and 20 to the students and then ask them to compare Kevin's home life with that of Salom's.

Students should point out that Salom has no respect for his mother and Salom's father is a drunk who has no respect for his son. The family is clearly dysfunctional. Students should notice that Kevin, through Salom, is re-evaluating his own family situation, which appears better than Salom's situation. Salom feels that he's in the middle, between his arguing parents. This gives him a motive and reason for the way he is and for what he does. It does not give him an excuse!

I ask groups to think about Salom. What else do we learn about him in Chapter 19? The answer is in the warning given to Kevin from Salom's neighbour.

There is a mystery in Chapter 19. Who writes on the walls? Who is responsible for the metre-high letters that tell us Salom is evil?

Finally, ask the students to write a short essay entitled 'Salom, Mystery Solved'. The essay could include what happened to Stash and who is responsible for the lettering. Students could include Salom's home life. Why does his dad drink? Why is his mother so feeble? How did Salom lose respect for his mother?

Alternative writing or additional work could include a social report on Salom's home background. A social worker could have visited Salom and his parents and is now constructing a report. Although the report can add new information, students should find information from the text to support their writing.

Chapter 20 shows the reader that Kevin's parents care about him. They are seen in a positive light. There is a further contrast between his family and Salom's family.

The reader can see that Kevin has changed from the start of the novel. His attitude towards his parents has changed. Tommy also realizes that Kevin has changed.

As a task, students can continue Tommy's diary. They can write about what has happened to Glory, how Tommy is excluded by Kevin and how he believes Kevin has changed.

In Chapter 21 the reader's attitude towards Salom and Doc should have altered. The reader is now able to see both characters as they really are. Students can continue their character chart, putting in how they feel the characters have developed, with evidence from the text to support their views.

In Chapter 22 Kevin realizes Salom is a liar. Ask the students to write Kevin's diary. In his entry, Kevin would mention Salom's lies. Students can discuss the role of Glory in the novel. They should note that she adds humour to it. They should find two examples to support this. Glory also reveals things to Kevin that she has discovered. This is an author technique to bring attention to things that the reader needs to know.

By Chapter 23 and 24 there are still a lot of unanswered questions in this novel. How does Doc really end up in hospital? Was Salom involved? Why does Torry lie about the MacAfee event? Ask the students to bullet point questions they would like to ask certain characters.

In small groups, students can hot-seat Salom, Doc and Torry.

Chapters 25–29 conclude the novel. Chapter 28 is a very exciting part. In small groups, students can improvise and act out this chapter. At the end of the novel, ask students 'How do you feel about Kevin, Salom and Doc?' Students can also complete their character track and write a final diary entry from the point of view of one of the characters.

For further tasks, students can write a review of the novel. They should mention how much they enjoyed it. Which parts did they like best and why? Are there any parts of the novel they think could be improved? Which characters could they identify with and why? Did the plot work? Who would they recommend the novel to?

Friends
If the students had the chance to spend a day with one of the characters in *Tribes*, which one would they choose and why?

Your product
(This is a sure winner.)

Point out to the students that every year new products are placed on the market. Their task is to invent a new product that will make them a fortune.

Their first task is to do a class research and discover what people want. Where is there a gap in the market?

For instance, students can research on the internet, looking at what some people feel that others should or should not eat in this age. Jamie Oliver launched a campaign for healthy eating only a few years ago, and there is currently an obesity problem in our country. There has also been a concerted battle to stop people wearing animal fur. Students need to be aware of current issues when launching a product.

The students then need to invent their product. They then need to name it.

Example:
'Snappy Shoes'
Our shoes are awesome. There is no need to fiddle with shoelaces or buckles. All you do is put your shoes on your feet, wiggle your feet and the shoes snap shut. Great when you're in a hurry! The shoes don't come undone and there is no untying of knots in laces, either.

Activities
Students should prepare a press release for their new product. The press release should include:

- The name of the product.
- Some facts about the product – including why it differs from other products already on the market.
- Positive comments by people who have tried it.
- Ideas as to why the product will be a success (at the end).
- Details of a person to contact for further information.

Example

Snappy Shoes

Inventive Shoes, the manufacturer of innovative shoes, has launched an amazing shoe that it believes will be the most successful shoe ever invented.

This shoe differs from others in that the customer does not have to bother with laces, buckles or anything else. All customers need to do is wiggle their toes and the shoes snap shut.

Actor Alwyn Annand tried the shoes:

'They're amazing! I'm buying a pair, as soon as they reach the shops', he said.

For further information, contact Jade Wilson at Inventive Shoes Ltd, Fair Tread Road, Steppington ST12 3SH. Or visit our website at www.inventiveshoes.co.uk

After this work is complete, ask the students to read the following and the report from a national newspaper. This is also available online.

Financial disaster

Your product has become involved in a health and safety issue. You know that to withdraw your product would involve the company going bust and many workers would be unemployed. You need to do something! Read the newspaper article below and tackle the issue.

Shoe health hazard

Many of today's new shoes are unfit to wear. Years ago, shoes were tested with care and they lasted for years.

Some unscrupulous manufacturers bring out new products before they are fully tested. The new type of shoe that snaps onto your feet is a typical example. The product was launched quickly and was available in our shops within weeks.

Today, a young girl lies in a hospital bed; a victim of a shoe-related accident. She had bought shoes that forced her to walk on the tips of her toes. She tripped on the pavement and sustained a broken ankle. There have been other serious accidents throughout the country. These accidents are caused by ill-fitting shoes.

The new type of shoe should be banned and withdrawn from our shops immediately.

Tell the students that they are responsible for the product 'Snappy Shoes'. In small groups, they should make a list of things they intend to do to safeguard the sale of the shoes. They might like to think about the following points:

- Improve factory safety checks on the shoes.
- Make some adjustments to 'Snappy Shoes'.
- Write a letter to the national newspaper expressing the company's point of view. (How do they know wearing 'Snappy Shoes' caused the accidents?)

As a further exercise, ask the students to look at their invented product and write a newspaper article condemning their product.

It might be desirable for the students to design and draw their product before engaging with the written work. This would make a useful homework.

Traditional version versus modern version

Another interesting English lesson, that the vast majority of students enjoy, is turning a well known fairy tale into a modern version. As a modelling exercise, read the students the following two versions of the same tale.

Beauty and the Beast – traditional version

A rich merchant has three daughters. All are good looking and the youngest is so attractive she's known as Beauty. The other two sisters are jealous of Beauty because she's more attractive than they are.

The merchant's business fails and the family are suddenly made poor. All the money has gone and they have to live a different lifestyle. The merchant father decides to go on a trip to see if he can find new wealth. The spoiled older sisters expect fine clothes but Beauty asks only for a rose.

The merchant does not find new wealth on his travels and he wanders into a forest when he is caught in a snowstorm. He discovers a seemingly deserted palace where he finds food and shelter for the night. In the morning, he wanders into a large garden and finds a rose there. He plucks the rose for Beauty and intends to go home. Suddenly, a frightful beast appears. The Beast tells the merchant he must die for his theft. The merchant begs for his life.

'Only if you let me have one of your beautiful daughters as my wife,' said Beast.

The merchant agreed, knowing that if he refused he would die and his daughters would starve. Beast gives the merchant a chest filled with gold and shows the merchant how to get home.

On arriving home, the merchant gives Beauty the rose.

'Sadly, there's a slight snag,' said the merchant. 'A beast appeared and told me I'd die unless you are given to him.'

'Then I have to go and be with Beast,' said Beauty, as tears fell from her unhappy face.

Her father promised to take her to Beast's castle and leave her there. He dumped his daughter by the castle walls and ran off as fast as he could.

That night Beauty dreams she sees a beautiful lady who thanks her for her sacrifice, telling her she will not go unrewarded. She is left alone all day and soon becomes bored. Every evening she has supper with Beast. Because she is so lonely, Beauty looks forward to her meetings with Beast in the evening and eating and talking with him.

One evening Beast asks her to marry him.

'I'm sorry, I cannot do that, I don't know you that well. I don't love you,' says Beauty.

The following evening, Beast looks very unhappy.

'I have looked into my magic mirror and I see your father is very ill. He misses you so much.'

Beauty bursts into tears.

'Please let me visit my poor father,' she begs.

Beast can see Beauty is unhappy.

'You can visit your dad but if you don't return in a week, I'll die!' Before Beauty can reply, Beast has walked quickly from the room.

Beauty enjoys being back with her family and nurses her father back to health. Her sisters are jealous of her and the fact that she has everything money can buy. They persuade her to stay on, thinking the Beast will forget all about her. Then Beauty has a dream. She sees Beast dying of a broken heart. She realizes, ugly as he is, that she loves him. She rushes back to the castle and does indeed find Beast dying of a broken heart. She kisses him and he instantly turns into a handsome prince.

Beauty marries her prince and they live a long and happy life because their love is founded on goodness.

(Author's interpretation)

The modern version will change the character of Beauty.

Beauty and the Beast – modern version

A merchant has three daughters, two are quite attractive but the third is ugly.

'Ha, let's call this one Beauty, yuck she's so gross,' said a sister. The other sister agreed and the name stuck.

The merchant was rich until he invested in silly things, such as trying to discover new planets in the solar system. He soon lost all his dosh. The family became poor. The merchant decided to travel to see his investors and reclaim some money. Before he went, he asked the sisters what they wanted – the older two asked for the usual wish-list of a new car each. Beauty wanted a luxury yacht, she'd seen one called 'The Rose'. Trust her dad to get the wrong end of the stick, which is a thorny subject, as we shall see!

Dad failed in his quest to borrow loads of money because of the credit crunch and had to return with nothing. His map-reading abilities were poor and he didn't have sat nav, so he got lost in a forest. To make matters worse, it snowed by the bucket-full. He found his way to a palace and found food in the larder. He also noticed a rose garden and picked the biggest rose for his ugly daughter.

'Anything to please one of them', he muttered.

Just then Beast arrived on the scene. This guy was covered in acne, had large pussy spots all over his hideous face, was squinty-eyed and his breath stank.

He threatened to kill the merchant, who was thinking it's better to be a live coward rather than a dead hero. He offered his daughter, named Beauty. Beast thought Beauty would be – well, beautiful. He offered the merchant a bag of gold and told him to bring Beauty to the palace as soon as possible.

The merchant gave Beauty the rose and told her everything.

'Dream on, dad. I'm not saving your life. My sisters and I can divide the gold and live a good life eating the best food, binge drinking, throwing up all over town and enjoying life to the full.'

The sisters overheard Beauty's conversation and decided to spike her drinks that night. So Beauty ended up outside the castle while Beast looked down on her.

Beauty met Beast for supper that evening.

'You're an ugly big monster,' she screeched as she tucked into all the rich food on offer.

'You can talk,' said Beast, as he ate his food.

The next morning, Beauty weighed herself and discovered she'd put on a few pounds from all the food she'd devoured, but she never learned her lesson. Soon she became as large as a balloon.

Beast had to get rid of this ugly ungrateful and spoilt younger daughter of a merchant. He looked into the cracked mirror, it had cracked when he'd first looked into it!

'Ah, this mirror is magic. You're dad's missing you, you'd better go!' he insisted.

Beauty smiled and burped. 'Not so fast, I'm here to stay, you great oaf. That mirror ain't magic anyway. You're trying to get rid of me!'

Beast smiled, showing a row of blackened teeth.

'Marry me, then!'

Beauty spat out an apple pie that was lurking in the corner of her large mouth.

'Marry you, you large lump of shifty-eyed jelly. You're joking!' Beauty stormed out of the room and ran upstairs to pack her bags.

Back home, things were awful. She was forced to work for a living, endure her sister's taunts about her weight issues and watch while they dated all the handsome men in the village.

'Huh! I'm better off with Beast,' she grumbled as she re-packed her bags and wobbled off to the castle. She found Beast alone in his castle. He'd been jilted by the local barmaid. He was dying of a broken heart.

Beauty kissed him. 'Hey, ugly mush, I'll have to do!'

Beast turned into a handsome prince and she . . . well, she just stayed as she was.

They married and had some sort of a life together.

Now ask the students to write their own modern version of a well-known fairy tale.

Soaps – for characters

This lesson will enable students to write about characters in an interesting way. Tell the students, 'Most of you will have watched 'EastEnders', 'Coronation Street', 'Home and Away' or another soap opera. You will know what soaps are all about.

Now imagine that a production company wants to launch a new soap opera named 'Laurel Avenue'. We are privileged in that we are able to have a sneak preview and see some of the characters and read about some of the storylines. We have also been asked to extend and develop some of the storylines. The characters and stories below are all available online.

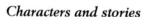

Characters and stories

- Miss Tina Almond – she runs the local post office and stores. She's a bit short-sighted and quite old, so she often confuses customers. However, she's sharp when it comes to the gossip. She knows it all!
- Next door to Miss Almond is the Yarker family. Tony and Wendy run the fish and chip shop and their daughter, Felicity, helps them. Their son, Grant, is at university – but Miss Almond has heard that he's dropped out of university and is living rough. Felicity also has a dark secret that her parents don't know. But Miss Almond knows . . . and she's about to reveal a secret that could ruin the Yarker family!
- Liz Asher lives next door. She's always seeing the doctor. Her husband, Alex, is packing his bags. He's about to walk out on Liz. He thinks she's a hypochondriac. However, she's just had the results of the hospital tests and she has some bad news for Alex.
- The Patel family, Naajy and Aamael, run the Indian restaurant and Aamael is expecting her first baby. She's been rushed to hospital. Naajy can't join her as a fire has just broken out at the restaurant.
- Doctor Sweetman is due to retire and he enjoys fishing. However, he's being blackmailed for something that happened in the past. Who is blackmailing him? He lives in a large house near the restaurant but his surgery is in the next street to Laurel Avenue.
- Joyce Easterway runs the local pub, The Nags Head. She is helped by Reg Gaudin, who also runs the local garage, Gaudin's Cheap Deals. Barmaids, Jane Smullen and Suzie Winward, also help out.

Joyce Easterway's ex-husband has just escaped from prison and is heading for Laurel Avenue. He is out to get Joyce, whom he blames for his imprisonment. Suzie is depressed because her boyfriend, Jamie Myatt, has walked out on her. Jamie, unknown to Suzie, is seeing her best friend, Jane. Jamie lodges with the doctor.

- Rory Drain is on the dole. He's always in the pub and trying to chat up Jane Smullen. She's either sarcastic to him or avoids him. He has usually found it difficult to pay his way. Suddenly, he is rich and able to splash his money around like water. Where did all the money come from? His dream is to visit the Greek island of Cos.
- Reverend Alicia Capman lives at the vicarage and the barmaids lodge with her. She invites all to her church teas but is she what she appears to be? The local newspaper journalist, Les Drummond, has hinted otherwise. He also lodges with her.

Tasks

Ask the students to choose the characters from 'Laurel Avenue' that they find the most interesting. They could think and then write about what the characters might say to each other when they meet. They should set their work out in play form.

Example

'Laurel Avenue'

Scene 1: The Nag's Head

(Rory Drain is slumped at the bar. He is watching Jane Smullen closely. She is aware that he's watching her.)

Rory *(to Jane)*: Here, buy yourself something nice, eh? *(He throws a pile of notes onto the bar)* A gift from me, eh?

Jane *(quickly pockets the money)*: Where did you get all that dosh from, Rory?

Rory *(unconvincing)*: Eh? Money? Oh, I had a maiden aunt. The old bat liked me. Left me the lot when she died. Good, eh?

Jane *(suspicious)*: Where did she live? What did she do?

Rory *(sips glass of wine)*: Don't know, don't care. She left me the lot. A small fortune, eh?

(Doctor Sweetman walks in from the lounge)

Doctor: A glass of apple juice, please Jane.

Rory *(stands up straight)*: Ah, Doctor Sweetman. I've been expecting you. A word in your ear, a private word.

(Rory and the doctor go off to a distant table as Jamie walks in)

Jamie *(winks at Jane)*: The usual please, love!

Jane *(confidentially)*: You know, there is something going on between Rory and Doctor Sweetman. The Doc dosen't appear too happy . . .

(Suddenly, the pub door swings open. A tall, gaunt man stands in the doorway. He glares at everyone. They look into his bloodshot eyes and notice the stubble on his chin. He has a desperate look about him)

Pete: Where's Joyce Easterway? I want to see her now. I'm her husband, Pete.

Students can either continue the script (which is also available online) or write their own, using the characters involved in this soap. They should note that some soap storylines are deliberately misleading. For instance, it appears that Rory is the one who's blackmailing Doctor Sweetman. Evidence: Rory has gained money and Jane does not believe his tale about the maiden aunt. He is speaking to Doctor Sweetman in private. However, could there be other explanations? Are these two events a coincidence?

If they wish, students should be allowed to make up additional characters who live in the Avenue.

Tell the students that soaps never use just one storyline. There are usually a few storylines occurring at the same time and sometimes they interconnect . . . just like real life.

Finally, students can act out the scripts in groups. Those watching should comment on the storyline and the characters. They should give each group a mark out of ten.

The story

Each of the characters in 'Laurel Avenue' has a story to tell. What could happen next in 'Laurel Avenue'? How many possible storylines are developing? List some of the storylines that are hinted at as the characters are introduced.

Examples

- Grant could be in with bad company and about to get into serious trouble.
- Felicity might be the arsonist – she was bored and wanted excitement in her life. Miss Almond was watching her!
- Liz Asher might be seriously ill and her husband will have to make a choice – stay with her or go to his brother's house in London.
- The fire at the Patel restaurant needs to be dealt with. Does Naajy go to the hospital with his wife or does he risk his life to save his restaurant?

The students should now use bullet points and list further potential storylines for future development.

Finally, students can choose the storyline that appears to be the most interesting. They should decide where the events of the story will take place – in the restaurant, the post office, the chip shop or elsewhere. They should think about the characters, *what* they will say and *how* they will say their lines. How the characters will react as the story unfolds.

A comprehension to inspire less-able students

The purpose of this work is to develop the students' skills in reading and understanding. The following beginning of a story is also available online.

Trapped

The fairground rides whizzed around and the lights twinkled in the dark August night.

Wayne and Andrew had been on almost every ride. Wayne checked in his pockets. He had a one-pound coin, an old apple core and an elastic band. Only the pound was worth anything.

Wayne noticed a thin, old man who stood next to a funny looking machine. The machine gleamed like a spaceship.

The man wore a large, brown hat and he stroked his short, white beard. Then he rubbed his old hands and laughed loudly. Wayne did not like his laugh.

Andrew looked at the old man, he thought the man's eyes glowed orange, like a sunset . . . like his worn orange jacket. He had a yellow scarf wrapped around his neck and his oily trousers were a deep blue.

'Step inside my machine,' he said to the boys. 'Only a pound a go.'

'What does the machine do?' asked Andrew.

The old man laughed. His laugh made Wayne shiver.

'My machine will take you to different worlds,' answered the old man. He stroked his short, grey beard.

Wayne did not want to go inside the machine. He was afraid of the old man. Andrew took the pound coin from Wayne's hand. He gave the money to the old man. The old man looked at the coin and placed it inside the pocket of his blue trousers.

'There are different worlds inside my machine,' said the old man. 'You might think you are back in your world, but you won't be. You can both have a ride for the one pound.'

He laughed as the boys stepped inside the machine.

Ask the students to answer the following questions:

1. What three things did Wayne have in his pocket?
2. What did Wayne dislike about the old man?
3. What does the machine do?
4. What does the old man look like?
5. What do you think will happen next?

Tell the students to write about the old man's appearance. Tell them the chart below, which is also available online, will help them.

He wore a large, _____ _____ and he had a short, _____.
His eyes were _____ and he wore a yellow _____.
His jacket was _____ and his trousers were _____.

Further activities could include the following.

Reading and speaking
Ask the students to re-read 'Trapped' and make a list of the main events in the story. They can now take it in turns to retell the story – just looking at the list they have made.

Speaking and listening
Ask the students to form small groups and think about any science fiction stories or strange stories they have heard about. They can tell their story to the rest of the group.

Developing the story further
Ask the students to think about what might happen next. They can look at the list of suggestions and take up one suggestion to continue the story.

- Wayne and Andrew climb out of the machine. Everything is the same. The old man has taken their pound. The whole thing was a hoax.
- When Wayne and Andrew climb out of the machine, there are armed troops waiting for them. The troops all have orange eyes.
- The machine crashes and Andrew is injured. Wayne helps his friend out of the machine. They have landed in a world full of icebergs and ice-mountains. Heading towards them are alien creatures.
- When Wayne and Andrew climb out of the machine, they think the whole thing was a hoax, everything looks almost the same . . . but everyone has large green eyes! The old man's scarf is blue and not yellow. His hat is a large, black stetson.

Using the story as a stimulus for improving English
Revise the use of sentences with the students.

Tell them that when they write they must use sentences or people will have difficulty understanding what they have written. Ask them to decide which of the following are sentences and then ask them to write out the complete sentences and make the incomplete ones into proper sentences.

- Wayne and Andrew had been.
- Wayne checked in his pockets.
- The man wore.
- The machine was like a spaceship.
- Wayne did not like.
- The old man laughed.

Next tell the students there are some jumbled sentences. Some of the words are the wrong way around. They need to re-write the sentences so that they make sense. The sentences below are also available online.

- it was scary. because the story I liked
- not very brave. Wayne was
- bravest boy in the story. the Andrew was
- funny clothes. The wore old man
- different worlds. takes you to The machine
- inside the machine. I would not step

Ghost stories

Students love writing ghost stories. As mentioned previously, they usually have a few to tell. Following is an example to help stimulate their ideas. It is also available online.

The Attic

Jane and Harry had always thought that the attic was a gloomy place. It was a place only seen in torchlight and there were strange shadows lurking in dark corners. It was full of old junk from great-grandfather's time. There were old wooden chests and seafaring things such as old spyglasses and ships' compasses. There were also old boxes and pieces of disused furniture, such as a chair with three legs and a rocking horse without a head. There was also a disused typewriter that was so rusty the keys failed to work.

Mum wanted the place cleared out and tidied. She wanted the place converted into an art studio. The builders were coming to put in a special window and plaster the walls. Mum had ordered Jane and Harry to bring the junk down from the attic and throw it all into a skip. The past was the past, she'd said. She wanted to start anew, make things bright and open and cheerful.

The day to remove the junk was a heavy rain-filled day. The wind blew and the whole house appeared to shake, shake like a sad old man burdened with some deep grief. Harry peered into the attic from the top of the ladder. The room at the top of the house seemed gloomier than ever. He shone his torch into the attic and stepped into the room. He walked over to the headless rocking horse. He grabbed the thing around its middle. The horse is worthless, he thought. He threw it across the floor, towards the entrance. It was then he heard a small croaky voice.

'What are you doing with my things?' it asked.

Harry could feel his skin prickle and his heart began to beat faster. He turned towards the place where the voice came from. Nothing, only a shaft of light that could have been the shape of an old man.

Ask the students to read the story; then ask the following questions:

- How does the start of the story introduce us to the idea that this could be a ghost story?
- What new information do we glean from the second paragraph?
- How does the third paragraph create suspense?
- Is the final paragraph a surprise?

Now ask the students to complete the story. They should think about what might happen next. Will Harry tell Jane all about what he'd heard and seen? Will she also see the ghost? How will Harry explain the events to his mother? What might be the outcome? Will they still clear out the attic or will they keep things as they are?

Ask the students to thought-shower for a possible ghost story. Following are some titles they could choose:

- The headless horseman;
- The secrets of Sundown Grange;
- A ghostly hitchhiker;
- Through the mist.

Working on their own, students can write their own ghost stories. Ghost stories work well with Year 7 and Year 8 students. There is an online resource for students who have difficulty thinking of plots.

Student-friendly news and newspapers

This is a lesson I used for many years. It does take some preparation and organization but the outcome is worthwhile.

Divide the class into small groups of about five or six. Then tell each group to pick an editor. The editor picks a sub-editor, a sports editor, a fashion editor and a gossip columnist. The editor can choose a cartoonist if one of the team can draw.

Then pick a member from each group who can be called upon to be a runner.

The first task for the students is to invent an interesting name for their newspaper. Then tell them the news of the day or show them the headlines on a screen. They need to discuss what they feel should go on the front and back pages of their newspaper. They also decide, as a group, what interesting pieces of gossip are to go into the newspaper. They need to appreciate that news is on the front page of a newspaper and sport is on the back. News can be political, dramatic or gossip – depending upon the type of newspaper they are producing.

The news of the day

- The American President is due to fly out from Washington to meet the British Prime Minister for crisis talks on the economy.
- Big Ben has broken down and needs urgent repairs.
- A dog has sniffed out a gang of jewel thieves.
- There has been a plane crash near Stratford-on-Avon. Survivors tell their stories.

Students need to write two or three of the stories and decide which one will make the front page! They need to know there might be breaking news, so they might have to re-write their stories.

The gossip of the day

- Football star, Greg Jakes, was seen talking to the manager of Real Madrid. Is he about to leave premiership leaders Middletown FC?
- Formula 1 Driver Geoff Collins has split up with his wife.
- Pop star Divine Glory has been rushed to hospital.
- David Storme, manager of Hill Town, has been sacked.

Sports news

- Rugby Union leaders Huddlestone were beaten 32–16 by Minnows Buxton last night.
- British tennis star, Jeanette Leeson, has reached the quarter finals of the French Open.
- British golfer, Mark Brick, has won a major tournament.

Allow the students to work on the newspaper for about 20 minutes. Then you call the runners and give them a sheet of paper each, with the breaking news.

Each group has to decide what to do with the breaking news. If they decide to take no action, their newspaper will be dated before it is printed. If they re-write their news headlines, that will need to be done quickly . . . before the end of the lesson.

Breaking news

- The American President is taken ill aboard Air Force One. He is rushed to hospital.
- There has been a train crash outside Swindon.
- Tennis star, Jeanette Leeson, has injured her knee while practising for the quarter finals. She might have to withdraw from her match against champion Nadine Zargova.

When presented with the breaking news, students will need to think quickly. They will need to decide which of the pieces of breaking news are important. Which will be their new headline? Which is the piece of news that will make the front page?

If you have an able class, you might like to introduce further breaking news in the last quarter of the lesson.

Further breaking news

- Emily Watkins has broken the world record for producing the most pancakes in an hour.
- There has been an earthquake in northern Greece. There are 34 known casualties.
- Pop star Maddie Ferguson has been arrested by police for causing a public disturbance.
- A dangerous snake has escaped from the local zoo.

Once again, the students need to decide if their headline page needs to change.

The students need to produce a rough draft of their newspaper by the end of the day. The following lesson, the newspaper needs to be produced using their IT skills.

The lesson enables students to work quickly as a team and make joint decisions. They also need to write quickly and carefully. This lesson can test their speaking and listening skills and their writing outcome.

Postcards home

I remember reading a postcard from my great-great aunt to my grandfather, when he was a young man. I started thinking what it might have been like if my great-grandfather had written to me, when he was a boy. What might he have said? What was important to him in his life? The postcard might have been something like as follows, which is also available online.

Northdown
Margate
Kent

18 July 1871

Dear Great-grandson,

I live in Margate but I'd like to see other places. When I'm older I'm going to work on the fishing fleets. My dad works on a farm but there isn't enough money in farming these days. You never know, I might end up in a big fishing place like Lowestoft.

I have one brother and he is named James William West. I think mum and dad ran out of ideas for names!

I read a book last week. It was by an author named Charles Dickens. He died last year and everyone is reading his books because he will not be writing any new ones. The book is called *Oliver Twist*. It is about an orphan boy. What sort of books do you read?

Our Queen is Victoria and I'm proud of Britain as we are the most powerful nation on Earth.

School is tough. If I can't work out my sums, I get four strokes of the cane.

I put my address on the postcard because I shan't post this card. I'll put it in **my** album for you to read when you reach 14.

My regards to you,

William James West

Read the letter to the students and ask them to research their family history. Ask them to imagine that their great-grandfather or great-grandmother has sent them a postcard. They have discovered the postcard.

The task is that they need to write the postcard, using any family information they have on their great-grandfather or great-grandmother. I discovered that my great-grandfather was born in Margate and that his father worked on a farm. I also knew that he went into fishing and moved to Lowestoft. I discovered that he had one brother with virtually the same name! The rest . . . I made up.

Students can then imagine that they can post through time. They can send a postcard to their great-grandparent. This is also available online.

Dear William (great-grandfather),

Many thanks for your postcard. We still read Charles Dickens' books.

You would not believe how life has changed since your time. We fly to other countries by aeroplane. We can get to America in 6 hours and to Australia in 1 day. We drive our cars on motorways. I live in Colchester and I can get to London by car in less than 2 hours. I can visit friends in Cambridge in about 1½ hours.

I have a computer which connects to something called the internet. I find all sorts of information on the internet and I can type a letter using my word processor. I can see my friends' photographs on 'Facebook', and keep in touch with them.

I'll tell you more when I have time to write you a letter.

Best wishes,

Keith (great-grandson)

A letter to your great-grandson

As a further task, ask the students to write a letter to their great-grandchild. Before doing so, they will need to imagine what life might be like in 100 years time. Will people be living in cities underground? This will avoid further damage to the environment and make it possible for more people to live on Earth. Will the planet be much warmer, due to the environmental damage we have made? Will pens be things of the past? Will there be any illnesses or will medical science have wiped out diseases?

Ask the students to read the following letter to the future, which is also available online.

> 16 Tamburlaine Avenue
> Colchester
> Essex
>
> 20 May 2010
>
> Dear Great-grandchild,
>
> Life here is awesome! I mean, I have my own laptop and access to the internet. Mum leaves me alone because she's too busy catching up with Aunt Jean on her mobile.
>
> I microwave my food, feed Podge, our pet dog, and then go around the block to see my mates – but only if I'm not in the mood for my laptop.
>
> Then there're soaps to watch, 'EastEnders' is my favourite, it's fab. There are a lot of exciting storylines and characters.
>
> I often watch the sport's channel. Chealsea are magic. They're going to win the Premiership title again this season . . . I hope.
>
> Have a great life.
>
> Your future great-grandmother,
>
> Arlene

Ask the students to look through the letter and pick out words and phrases that a great-grandchild might not understand.

They should pick out the following: awesome; laptop; internet; mobile; around the block; mates; soaps; 'EastEnders'; fab; Chelsea (possibly).

Considering how things might have changed over the years, the students should take care to mention their lives, their hobbies and their interests. They should explain everything carefully.

Following is an example from a Year 7 student.

12 St Luke's Drive
Burfields
Callie Town
CT1 3IR

Dear Great-grandchild,

I want to tell you all about myself and my life at the moment.

I live with my older brother and younger sister. My mum looks after us both. We live in a semi-detached house in a village called Burfields. Our dad doesn't live with us and we see him every other weekend. He lives and works in the near-by town of Crosschester.

My friends and I go to the local school, which is a large comprehensive. We catch a bus to get there.

These days we are all worried about global warming and the effects it might have on you. Places like London and some of the coastline around Britain might have disappeared by your time.

My ambition is to be an ice-skater when I grow up. I practise at the local ice-rink three evenings a week.

If you read this letter and can time travel, do come and visit.

All the best,

Chloe Gordimer

Ask the students to write their letter to the future. As an additional exercise, ask them to write a reply from their great-grandchild. They will need to use their imaginations for this one. Below is an example from a Year 8 student.

34 Undersea Drive
New Town
Maxi-Zone 7

4 May 2110

Dear Great-grandad,

Well, we can't time travel yet. However, we can post letters through time, so enjoy!

I don't know if you ever got to drive fly-cars but dad drives us from England Undersea to Australia Undersea in about 2 hours. I'm able to see my cousins for a few days before we drive home.

Home is an underground city named Maxi-Zone. We live in Maxi-Zone 7. When I leave the city and come up on ground, I see Earth full of trees and singing birds and animals. All the houses you built in your time are demolished and nature has taken over.

The underground cities were built to reverse the effects of global warming by planting lots of trees. When London flooded and the

Houses of Parliament were destroyed, the governments of the world decided that drastic action was needed.

I hate living like a rabbit in an underground house but I think it is better than the world being destroyed.

School finished about 30 years ago and we now do individual learning at home. If I fail my exams, I can't come up on Earth for a month. So I'm working hard to pass everything!

We don't keep pets anymore but the rats are everywhere. They are a modern problem.

I can't say if life is better or worse than in your time. Maybe one day I'll find out . . . when we've finally solved the problem of time travel!

Best wishes,

Sam O'Brien

Now ask the students to write their letter to the future.

The lesson is an interesting way to introduce the students to postcard and letter writing. They will know how to write postcards and friendly letters and they will have enjoyed the work in the process of learning.

Wordbag

In this exercise, students are presented with words and asked to make a story using the words given. They can work alone or in small groups.

This activity is similar to the poetry stimulus exercise on page 50. It allows students to add their own words, especially connectives. They are presented with new vocabulary and given the chance to use dictionaries if they wish. As with the poetry exercise, you cannot assume that all students are bursting with creativity and wanting to show you their amazing stories. Some are, many are not!

Inform the students that the wordbag has arrived but you have dropped it and words have spilled out everywhere. You can either cut up the words and place them in a large bag, then spill the words out on their desks or you can use the whiteboard to display the words. Again, students appear to react well to the seemingly random nature of the wordbag!

Students need to look at the words and think of their own title for a story. Below are some words that have worked for me. These are also available online.

Murky Illegal Smuggler Stowaway Shipwreck Lighthouse Captain Seasick Swim Shore Contraband Silk Cutlass Fight Rocks Gold Washed Up Hid Soldiers Dark Fearful Night Lantern Cave Spy Sprightly Echo Crashing Lookout Land Treacherous Pathway Escape Scar Captive Wailing

Following are two responses from two Year 9 students. Both are the first two paragraphs of a longer story.

The captain steered the ship through the murky waters. He knew he was carrying illegal contraband. He knew that he was a smuggler and that the coastguards were after him.

The ship hit a rock. It swayed dangerously. There hadn't been a warning light from the old lighthouse. The captain drew his cutlass and placed it between his teeth. If he had to swim for shore and meet the enemy, he wouldn't die without a fight.

By Nathaniel Smithers (Year 9)

The night was stormy. The sea was choppy. I saw the waves lash against our small boat. I knew we'd sink. Watching the waves made me feel seasick so I turned away.

I noticed the captain urgently talking to his men. As a stowaway, I needed to keep still.

Soldiers were running onto the sand. The shore was covered with redcoats. They were armed. Some were holding lanterns and waiting for our boat to sink, as it must! I was scared. If we made it ashore, they'd kill us. They knew we were smugglers.

By Tasha Jones (Year 9)

Starter lessons (or revision exercises)

Starters should be used at the beginning of a lesson to make students think and to prepare them for the main body of the lesson. Starters do not necessarily have to relate to the main body of a lesson. They can be a learning activity in their own right.

Students should be told immediately that starters will last no longer than 15 minutes and that there is a definite time allocation for them. The idea is for them to work and learn fast, before they start the main body of the lesson.

Following are four starters that have worked for me.

The connectives story

For this activity, you will need to display 20 connectives on a whiteboard. Students then need to divide into small groups of about four or five. They then need to form a story starting each new sentence using a connective from the list below. When they have written their stories, ask some of the students to read them out. Then ask the group to tell you where each connective was used in the story. Did the different connectives make the story more interesting?

I have used this exercise with Years 7–9 students and some lower-ability GCSE groups. It works well as it stops students using words such as then, so or and. The words below are also available online:

Once upon a time Alternatively For instance Similarly
Afterwards Although Meanwhile Furthermore
Just then As if Due to Without doubt
Because of this At that moment Since then Until then
Therefore After that Because of Then the

Completing sentences

When starting a sentence using i, a capital letter is needed. Students need to change the small i into a capital I and complete the sentences. You need to point out that the pronoun I always needs a capital letter, even in the middle of a sentence. For example: 'The shopping list, I had forgotten all about the shopping list!'

I have used this exercise with Year 7 students and with lower-ability Years 8 and 9 students. It is a useful exercise in that it reinforces the use of the capital I.

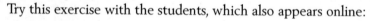

Try this exercise with the students, which also appears online:

- i think that . . .
- i am buying . . .
- i went to . . .
- i have a new . . .
- i am not . . .
- i hope that . . .
- i saw . . .
- i felt that . . .
- i knew that . . .
- i asked the . . .

Plurals not apostrophes

In this exercise, students need to take the apostrophe out of some of the sentences below but not all! I have done this exercise with Years 7–9 students. The sentences below are also available online.

- Damien put's his shoes on.
- The market man sells apple's, pear's and plum's.
- The cow's calf had disappeared.
- Shirley bought two new pair's of jean's yesterday.
- Grandma's car was stolen.
- Pete's mate caught a giant fish.
- Oliver Gate's new book sold well.
- Leave's fell into the pond.
- The Wars of the Rose's killed many people.
- Her friend's cat had kittens.

Poem decision

In this exercise, students can look at the poem below and think of a word that can fill the gap. They need to remember that they might find alternatives to the original that could make sense, providing the whole poem makes sense. I have used this exercise for Years 7–11. However, this particular example is best used for Years 7–9. It's also available online.

The Lake Isle of Innisfree

I will arise and go now, and go to _____
And a small cabin build there, of clay and wattles _____
Nine bean-rows will I have there, a hive for the honey- _____
And live alone in the bee-loud _____

And I shall have some peace there, for peace comes dropping _____
Dropping from the veils of the morning to where the cricket _____
There midnight's all a glimmer, and noon a purple _____
And evening full of the linnet's _____.

I will arise and go now, for always night and _____
I hear lake water lapping with low sounds by the _____
While I stand on the roadway, or on the pavements _____
I hear it in the deep heart's _____.

By William Butler Yeats

After the students have completed this exercise, give them the last lines of the poem but make sure that the last lines are jumbled up. See if they can reconstruct the poem as it was originally.

Last words (jumbled up): glade, Innisfree, made, slow, bee, wings, day, shore, sings, core, glow, grey.

CHAPTER 8

For the older students

GCSE English: AQA

The new GCSEs for English will be different in that there will be a third GCSE called English Language. The students will either take only GCSE English or both GCSE English Language and English Literature.

I will focus on GCSE English Language, as it is the new examination. As this book goes to press, it appears that the new examination will be as follows:

- 40 per cent will be externally assessed.
- 60 per cent will be controlled assessment.
- 30 per cent will be spoken language and of this 20 per cent will be speaking and listening, 10 per cent will be a study of the spoken language.
- 70 per cent will be written language and of this 35 per cent will be writing and 35 per cent will look at studying the written language.

The study of the spoken language will focus on the study of language variety, change and context. The study of the written language will include multimodal texts and one extended text. Writing will require students to write in a wide range of forms – looking at media, contexts, audience and purpose. The speaking and listening aspects will include real-life contexts in and beyond the classroom, and will expect students to employ a range of dramatic techniques and creative approaches.

The course on offer allows students to investigate and analyse language. Students are also able to experiment and use language creatively. This allows them to make 'fresh' and individual responses to each element of the assessment. The students will be encouraged to be imaginative and experiment with language to create interesting and original writing. I believe that, after years of 'dumbing down' the creative element at KS4, the new examination offers an exciting challenge.

The speaking and listening unit offers assessment on one activity for three categories:

- presenting;
- discussion and listening;
- role playing.

Offering guided lessons on all the changes is beyond the scope of this book but if we look at one aspect, writing in a wide range of forms, and if we take non-fiction, we can look at how the students can improve their grades.

The students can improve their grades by:

- Understanding the literal meaning of the texts. They also need to understand the texts' purpose and recognize their target audience. Students will need to point out how far the writers' aims are achieved. Crucially, the students will need to support their views by using evidence from the texts by quotations and examples.
- The students will need to distinguish between fact and opinion. It is worth pointing out that fact is something that can be proved to be true. They will usually find evidence to back-up the facts. Opinion is somebody's belief. It can be an interpretation of events.
- The students will need to follow an argument – this means knowing what the writer is trying to say and explain how the writer presents the arguments in the text. In some cases it is necessary to point out if the writer is implying anything in the argument. The important thing to get across to students is to show the examiner how the writer makes his/her points and how the argument progresses.
- The students will need to point out how the writer creates an effect – how is language used to create effect and who is it aimed at? Who is the audience and what is the purpose of the text?
- Finally, students will be required to comment on the layout and any other presentational devices – such as bullet points, pictures and subheadings.
- Below is a series of extracts from non-fiction texts that you can use to help your GCSE students understand the six points.

Fact and opinion

The cuckoo

Some species of cuckoo are known as parasitic. These nasty grey birds don't bother to rear their own young, but rudely dump their eggs in other birds' nests. The birds then raise the baby cuckoo as if it were their own. The cuckoo gets away with it, thus craftily avoiding the hassles of a hard-working parent.

Ask the students to work out what is fact and what is opinion in the above article, which is also available online. They should realize that 'nasty', 'rudely dump' and 'gets away with it' are the opinions of the writer, as is 'craftily avoiding the hassles'.

They also need to give an example of a fact, such as the other birds 'raise the baby cuckoo as if it were their own'.

Looking at audience and purpose

Following is an extract from a student's response which refers to the audience and purpose of the passage, which is also available online. The response below would give the student a good mark in the exam.

The writer's purpose is to persuade the reader that cuckoos are not pleasant birds. The writer uses words such as 'nasty' and 'crafty' and phrases such as 'rudely dumps' and 'gets away with it' to persuade us that cuckoos are lazy.

Exam practice

Students do not respond well to working on and going through endless past papers before taking their GCSE examinations. It is more effective to focus on some areas of the exam and give them snippets or short extracts. For example, why not look at similes, metaphors, alliteration and onomatopoeia in non-fiction texts? Most students are trained to look at these linguistic devices when analysing poetry – but many students fail to realize that these devices are also used in non-fiction texts. For example, the following extract from a ficticious autobiography includes examples of them all!

I was locked in the coalhouse. I felt like a trapped miner and smelt like a spent racehorse. I had no idea of how long I'd been there. For something to do in the pitch blackness, I counted the little lumps of loathsome coal. I screamed for the tap tap of shoes in the scullery and the click of the rusty key in the old lock. It was an eternity of waiting.
By Brian Tucker

To gain an A grade, the students should write something like:

The author makes his captivity in the coalhouse very vivid. He does this by using a series of linguistic devices. First of all, he uses two similes, which stress how he feels in the coalhouse: 'like a trapped miner' and 'a spent racehorse'. The second simile gives us an insight into his personal hygiene as he languishes in the coalhouse. We gain the impression that he has been in the coalhouse for some time.

The writer uses alliteration to inform the reader as to what he is reduced to doing in the dark, while he waits for his release: 'Counted the little lumps of loathsome coal.' The writer uses onomatopoeia as he screams for his freedom: 'tap tap of shoes' and 'click of the rusty key'. The fact that he screams emphasizes the plight of his situation.

Finally, the metaphor 'eternity of waiting' suggests that he has been locked in the coalhouse for a long time. It begs the question that must have been uppermost in his mind: will he ever be released?

The answer is an A-grade answer in that the linguistic devices are not only identified but discussed. The writer has a reason for using such devices and the student has identified these reasons. The answer is not generalized, but focuses on precise aspects of the language.

Looking at stylistic techniques

The students should note that a variety of stylistic techniques are used in non-fiction. It depends upon whether a writer of a text is attempting to persuade, argue, advise, inform, explain, describe, review or analyse. Again, providing a snippet giving brief examples and expecting the students to write a short response are best for revision purposes.

Ask the students to look at the extract from a newspaper article below – but before doing so, remind them of the techniques they are trying to spot and comment on. These are:

Rhetorical questions – usually added for impact, e.g. 'Can we really believe this?'

Emotive language – which is meant to touch the readers' feelings, e.g. 'These cute creatures are small and vulnerable and at our mercy. They are almost extinct.'

Irony – clever mockery, e.g. 'Having listened to Mr Hawker, I really can believe that prisoners should eat bread crumbs and rot in their cells.'

Exaggeration (the example can also be a metaphor), e.g. 'The very rich sail away from life's problems in their luxury yachts.'

Contrast, e.g. 'The enemy celebrate as our soldiers die.'

Colloquial language – which is like people chatting with each other, e.g. 'Impress me next time you wanna try and become Mr Big. Buzz off and take your puny mate with you!'

Ambiguity – where there is likely to be more than one interpretation. Ambiguity often looks like fact but could be used as sarcasm. For example, to suggest a boring pastime, e.g. 'Fishing is a lively and exciting pastime.'

Inference – things are suggested rather than stated, e.g. 'They felt
   guilty about the way they treated us. We never saw them again!'
Humour, e.g. 'My pet hamster is more dynamic than our science
teacher.'

The following extract is from a ficticious newspaper article, which is
also available online. It is brief but does use some of the techniques
above. Ask the students to spot as many as they can and comment upon
the reason or use of the techniques they spot.

> Can we put up with ill discipline in schools? I have always thought it an
> excellent idea to give kids the reward of a day or two at home when they
> misbehave. If you want them to cause havoc down town with their mates,
> give them the free time they need. Reward bad behaviour!
>
> When I was at school, back in the 1960s, misbehaving Dave got six strokes
> of the cane. He didn't misbehave after that!
>
> While hard-working kids slave over their maths papers, the disrespectful few
> enjoy the delights of kicking down garden gates or nicking goods from a poor
> shopkeeper in town. Do you know, there is more common sense in a garden
> slug than in some educationalists? All these kids need, to bring them round,
> is effective discipline.

A student aiming for a high grade might write something like the
following:

> The writer begins with a rhetorical question and asks us if we can 'put up with
> ill discipline in schools'. This suggests that there is widespread ill discipline
> in our schools. It also implies that something should be done about it. The
> writer uses irony, suggesting that naughty students are rewarded for their
> misbehaviour – 'A day or two at home.'
>
> The writer then suggests that students who are suspended from school 'cause
> havoc down town'. The writer uses colloquial language to engage the reader,
> such as: 'with their mates' and 'misbehaving Dave'.
>
> There is an implication that if a student is caned, as in the old days, the
> problems in schools would be solved: 'He didn't misbehave after that!'
>
> There is a suggestion that ill-disciplined students are having fun while hard-
> working students are somehow punished by slaving 'over their maths papers'.
> The writer ends with humour to reinforce criticism of the educationalists who
> shape school policy: 'There is more common sense in a garden slug.'
>
> The humour used is really a snipe at those who are in the forefront of the
> educational system: 'than in some educationalists'.
>
> Basically, the writer wants a return to some golden age where everyone
> worked and nobody messed about because they were afraid of corporal
> punishment. Surely this golden age never did exist!
>
> The short article is not backed up with any real evidence and is only using

the opinion of the writer. It appeals to those who believe things were better in the past. It also makes assumptions that those who are suspended for bad behaviour in schools are automatically stealing from shops or 'kicking down garden gates'.

The students should note that the language is analysed here to explain the writer's style. The writer's view is also interpreted and commented upon. The student has also used quotations to back-up the points made.

When thinking about how to tackle this type of question, tell the students to think 'a forest'.

A F O R E S T

Alliteration, fact, opinion, rhetorical questions, exaggeration, statistics, triplets (three)

There is an online resource for looking at magazine articles.

A brief look at the A-level syllabus (AQA)

The present and still comparatively new A-level examination expects students to read widely and use the information they have gained in an interesting way. It is not the scope of this book to go through the whole syllabus, but I have chosen two out of three options to look at. If we glance at Option A, Victorian Literature, we discover that the examination board expects students to link ideas and themes. It is called contextual linking. Following is a possible question that could be asked in the examination:

- Read the following extract carefully. It has been adapted from *The Moral and Physical Conditions of the Working Classes* by James Phillips Kay-Shuttleworth. It was published in 1832. In this extract, Shuttleworth expresses his views and observations of working-class life and conditions in Manchester.
- In your answer you should:
  - Consider the writer's thoughts and feelings about aspects of Victorian life and the ways in which he expresses them.
  - Compare this extract with your wider reading, pointing out how typical you think it is of Victorian literature. You should comment on both subject matter and style.

The introduction into this country of a singularly malignant contagious malady [cholera] which, though it selects its victims from every order of society, is chiefly propagated among those whose health is depressed by disease, mental anxiety, or want of the comforts and conveniences of life, had directed public attention to an investigation of the state of the poor. In Manchester, Boards of Health were established, in each of the fourteen districts of Police, for the purpose of minutely inspecting the state of houses and streets.

The township of Manchester chiefly consists of dense masses of houses, inhabited by the population engaged in the great manufactories of the cotton trade. Some of the central divisions are occupied by warehouses and shops, and a few streets by the dwellings of some of the more wealthy inhabitants; but the opulent merchants chiefly reside in the country, and even superior servants of their establishments inhabit the suburban townships. Manchester, properly so called, is chiefly inhabited by shopkeepers and the labouring classes. Those districts where the poor dwell are of very recent origin. The rapid growth of the cotton manufacture has attracted hither operatives from every part of the kingdom, and Ireland has poured forth the most destitute of her hordes to supply the constantly increasing demand for labour.

By James Phillips Kay-Shuttleworth

 The above extract is also available online.

How does a student tackle such a question? The student needs to be aware that the question is in two parts. The student will also need to use prior knowledge of Victorian life, picked up by a wide range of reading of both fiction and non-fiction, guided by yourself.

The first part of the question, though, is just concentrating upon the extract. So what are the writer's thoughts and feelings in what is essentially a factual report?

Shuttleworth has noted that cholera is widespread among the poor. He has given his reasons for the spread of cholera in the working-class areas of Manchester. The reasons are that 'health is depressed' by the spread of other diseases, which makes the victim weak and prone to further disease. Because the working classes are poor, they are subject to mental anxiety – for instance they may worry about how they are going to feed a large family if they have no money. According to Shuttleworth, they are bereft of the 'comforts and conveniences of life'.

Due to the rapid spread of cholera, Shuttleworth has noted that richer members of public intend to 'investigate the state of the poor'. He points out how the Boards of Health were established in Manchester and how the investigations will take place.

The second part of his writing focuses on the types of houses that existed in Manchester, 'dense mass of houses' and the types of trade that were carried on in central Manchester.

Finally, Shuttleworth tells us about the population shift into Manchester in order that the cotton trade had enough labourers. Here, he personifies Ireland as a woman: 'poured forth the most destitute of her hordes'.

He also implies that Ireland has dumped the worst of her kind on Manchester, which has exacerbated the problem.

Although the piece is mainly factual, we are given the impression, reading the piece as a whole, that Shuttleworth cares about the conditions of the working classes and intends to raise the awareness through his report. He does not dwell on his personal thoughts and feelings and the work is expressed as a factual report. However, he would not write this report if he did not care about the conditions of the poor in large city areas.

To gain a good result, students then need to compare this extract with work from their wider reading of Victorian literature. The wider reading could be from fiction or non-fiction. I suggest that you guide the students to read a variety of both. Reading should include newspaper extracts and letters. I further suggest that you guide them to such work as *Jane Eyre* by Charlotte Brontë and *Hard Times* by Charles Dickens. Both novels deal with Victorian issues. Among other themes, *Jane Eyre* deals with the following:

- bullying;
- attitudes towards God;
- adoption;
- deprivation;
- harsh conditions;
- the supernatural;
- marriage;
- death.

The Lowood chapters of *Jane Eyre* (Chapters 5–10) would be particularly appropriate for comparing conditions in the school with Shuttleworth's observations of Manchester. Following is a short extract from Chapter 9.

> That forest – dell, where Lowood lay, was the cradle of fog and fog-bred pestilence; which, quickening with the quickening spring, crept into the orphan Asylum, breathed typhus through its crowded school-room and dormitory, and, ere May arrived, transformed the seminary into a hospital.
>
> Semi-starvation and neglected colds had predisposed most of the students to receive infection: forty-five out of the eighty girls lay ill at one time.

Hard Times: fiction is Dickens' way of pointing out the harsh conditions of a manufacturing town.

Following is a short extract, which also appears online, from Chapter 5, where Dickens is describing Coke Town.

> It was a town of red brick, or of brick that would have been red if the smoke and ashes had allowed it; but as matters stood it was a town of unnatural red and black like the painted face of a savage. It was a town of machinery and tall chimneys, out of which interminable serpents of smoke trailed themselves for ever and ever, and never got uncoiled. It had a black canal in it, and a

river that ran purple with ill-smelling dye, and vast piles of building full of windows where there was a rattling and a trembling all day long, and where the piston of the steam-engine worked monotonously up and down like the head of an elephant in a state of melancholy madness. It contained several large streets still more like one another, inhabited by people equally like one another, who all went in and out at the same hours, with the same sound upon the same pavements, to do the same work, and to whom every day was the same as yesterday and to-morrow, and every year the counterpart of the last and the next.

The students can use these two extracts to point out that Shuttleworth's piece was typical of Victorian literature in terms of subject matter. However, if they wish to point out that not all Victorians agreed with him or that some Victorians were unaware of the social conditions of the working classes, they can look at Prince Albert's speech, shown below and online, at Mansion House in 1850. Prince Albert was a sponsor and major planner of the Great Exhibition, which took place in London in 1850.

The products of all quarters of the globe are placed at our disposal, and we have only to choose which is the best and the cheapest for our purposes, and the powers of production are entrusted to the stimulus of *competition and capital.*

So man is approaching a more complete fulfilment of that great and sacred mission which he has to perform in this world. His reason being created after the image of God, he has to use it to discover the laws by which the Almighty governs His creation, and, by making these laws his standard of action, to conquer nature to his use; himself a divine instrument.

Science discovers these laws of power, motion, and transformation; industry applies them to raw matter, which the earth yields us in abundance, but which becomes valuable only by knowledge. Art teaches us the immutable laws of beauty and symmetry, and gives our productions forms in accordance to them.

If I wanted to prepare my students for the examination, I would give them the Dickens extract and Prince Albert's speech. Price Albert's speech is about the finished product, which is beautiful. However, competition and capital mean that the product has to be made in the cheapest and best possible way. This means that workers are paid poorly and live and work in appalling conditions, which is pointed out in the Dickens extract.

The next step would be to discuss the Brontë extract and then give students the mock question paper. They would then have enough material to answer the question. For style, point out the format from my GCSE example above.

It is important for the students that you point out the importance of commenting on the typicality of a piece of writing. You need to guide the students to explore this.

Looking at Section B, which has a focus on World War I literature, students are often asked to compare two or more poems in some way. They need to comment on the issue in question, focusing on typicality and tone. They should also comment on style and use of language. Depending upon the phrasing of the question, different issues may need addressing. However, it is important to reinforce to students that comparison of the poems is central to the essay. The examiner will look for their ability to comment on the similarities, differences and overall effect.

For the purpose of this book, I will focus on preparing students for comparing poems. Obviously, they need to know about World War I from looking at diaries and literature as well as a range of other poems written during the war. They also need to be aware of the assessment objectives, so that they are clear as to what they are being assessed on.

When confronted with a comparison, students need to focus on why they are being asked to compare the two poems:

- Is it because of the style, the content or both?
- Is there a poem out of the two that appears more interesting or easier to understand?
- What are the different merits of both poems?
- Does one poem appear more accessible but have less depth?

When the students are clear in their minds concerning the above questions, they should open their essay with a clear introduction. The introduction should include the main focus and an outline of each poem.

When writing, students should be aware that their answer is relevant to the question. Unless stated in the question, students should write about each poem, giving equal space to each one. It is impossible to gain good marks if a student does not write an equal amount about each poem.

As students end their essays, they should conclude their thoughts and sum up the main points of the comparison.

To allow the students to understand the principles of comparison, try 'Peace' by Rupert Brooke and 'Anthem for Doomed Youth' by Wilfred Owen. Both are also available online.

Peace

Now, God be thanked Who has matched us with His hour,
And caught our youth, and wakened us from sleeping,
With hand made sure, clear eye, and sharpened power,
To turn, as swimmers into cleanness leaping,

Glad from a world grown old and cold and weary,
Leave the sick hearts that honour could not move,
And half-men, and their dirty songs and dreary,
And all the little emptiness of love!

Oh! We, who have known shame, we have found release there,
Where there's no ill, no grief, but sleep has mending,
Naught broken save this body, lost but breath;
Nothing to shake the laughing heart's long peace there
But only agony, and that has ending;
And the worst friend and enemy is but Death.

By Rupert Brooke (1914)

Anthem for Doomed Youth
What passing bells for those who die as cattle?
Only the monstrous anger of the guns.
Only the stuttering rifles' rapid rattle
Can patter out their hasty orisons.
No mockeries for them from prayers or bells,
Nor any voice of mourning save the choirs,–
The shrill, demented choirs of wailing shells;
And bugles calling for them from sad shires.

What candles may be held to speed them all?
Not in the hands of boys, but in their eyes
Shall shine the holy glimmers of good-byes.
The pallor of girls' brows shall be their pall;
Their flowers the tenderness of patient minds,
And each slow dusk a drawing- down of blinds.

By Wilfred Owen

Point out to the students that 'Peace' is a pro-war poem. In the first line, Brooke suggests that God 'has matched us with His hour'. The war, to Brooke, appears as a test from God, to see what the youth of his day were made of. Somehow the youth were sleeping. Now they are awake and better, they have been imbibed with 'sharper power'. He compares the youth with swimmers, who have turned into cleaner water. It is as if the youth were wasting their lives and going in the wrong direction. War has given them the opportunity to change direction and become heroes.

As with former poets of another age (such as Shakespeare's *Henry V* Agincourt speech) Brooke evokes honour: 'Leave the sick hearts that honour could not move.' Here, Brooke suggests that those who do not volunteer to fight for their country are dishonourable.

Brooke suggests that those who do not fight for their country are 'half-men' who entertain themselves singing 'dirty songs'. Those left behind are condemned to a 'dreary' life. They will be unfulfilled because their lives will remain empty. He even describes love as empty.

Brooke's youths have known shame but fighting the enemy, gaining honour and glory are described as 'a release'.

Sleep is used again but this time sleep suggests death: 'No grief but sleep has mending.'

Brooke further suggests that even the agony of a wound has an ending. Here he personifies death: 'And the worst friend and enemy is Death.'

Death is personified as a friend, taking the dying soldier into a better place. This takes the fear and ugliness out of death. Death is also seen as an enemy, taking the soldier from life.

The poem was written to persuade Britain's youth to volunteer and fight the war. Brooke could not know or understand the horrors of trench warfare. He died before poets such as Sassoon and Owen could write about the realities of war from the trenches. Brooke was brought up in schools where war was idolized and Latin poems were taught. Poets such as Horace were studied. These poets glorified war.

'Anthem for Doomed Youth' was written by Wilfred Owen, who was fighting in the trenches. He knew from first-hand experience the horror and reality of war. The first line of his poem mentions the dead soldiers. Owen suggests that the only passing bells for the dead are 'the monstrous anger of the guns'. The passing bells were funeral bells for remembrance. Soldiers in the trenches die and are forgotten about immediately, as the enemy guns are still firing. There is no dignity for the dead. Owen understands that death is ugly and not glorious, 'die as cattle' – cattle are killed in slaughter houses. To die as cattle depersonalizes the soldier. Death is on a mass scale – there will be no hero's recognition, which was promised and expected by those who studied Horace. Owen used alliteration to suggest the sound of the 'rifles' rapid rattle' which is also onomatopoeic and reproduces the sound of gunfire. The dead cannot get prayers. So many die that the orisons are 'hasty'.

When civilians die, prayers are said in churches; choirs sing songs. Owen describes the 'choir songs' as 'mockeries'. The 'choir songs' are shells, instruments of death. In war, the choirs are the 'wailing shells'.

Owen goes on to describe the sadness at home when a family member is killed in war: 'The pallor of girls' brows shall be their pall.' The girls have lost their boyfriends. The parents have only memories of their dead sons. The funerals attended were mockeries as they glossed over the reality of what was going on.

The two poems are very different, as Brooke is asking young men to enlist for a glorious fight that will rejuvenate them. Death is seen as a release or as glorious. Owen, on the other hand, is frank about the horrors and reality of war.

Please note: the work above is not intended as a comparison for

A-level purposes but, rather, is for the students to read and understand what they are meant to do when comparing and contrasting a poem.

Once they have studied the above, you can give them the following question:

- Compare and contrast four war poems that you have studied.

As a suggestion, they could choose two pro-war poems, such as 'England to Her Sons' by W.N. Hodgson and 'Peace' by Rupert Brooke. They could contrast these with two anti-war poems such as 'Air Raid' by Wilfred Gibson and 'Anthem for Doomed Youth' by Wilfred Owen.

If doing the above option, it is worth directing the students to Vera Brittain's 'Testament of Youth'. Vera Brittain was an educated female, not common in those days. She was able to recognize the reality of war to some extent. She can be contrasted with the poet Jessie Pope, who wrote pro-war propaganda poems. It is also worth directing the students to look at poems and letters from the beginning, middle and end of the war. The early poems suggest excitement and honour in fighting . . . and then disillusionment sets in! Poems looking at the war from hindsight are also interesting.

CHAPTER 9

Answers

Sentences (page 35)

- Belinda Blabbermouth tells everyone about *everything*.
- The dragon *destroyed* the village.
- Mrs Oldperson's clothes *stank* of mothballs.
- My horse is *called* Winraces.

Author's errors (page 35)

Stephen felt a hand on his shoulder. *He* knew he was in trouble. *He* heard the click of a gun. *There* was no way out of this mess. *Nothing* could save him now.

Capital letters (page 36)

- *Mrs* *T*oplady's head was bald.
- *J*ake lost money in *Las* *V*egas.
- *S*andra felt sick because she ate too many *E*aster eggs.
- *It* is fun to roam around *New* *Z*ealand.
- *The* wrestling champion from *B*irmingham is called *Luke* *N*oholds.

Full stops (page 36)

The gunman fired. Stephen fell to the ground. The gunman fled from the room. Stephen stood up. He felt dizzy but he was alive. The bullet-proof-vest had saved him.

Sentences ending in full stops, question marks or exclamation marks (page 36)

- Will it rain this afternoon?
- Come here!
- Yesterday it snowed heavily.
- Get inside this house!
- Did you hear about poor Annie?

Vowels (page 44)

My mate flew a kite, got hungry and went for a bite. He said he'd hate to dote on his sister's cute baby.

Empty House (page 56)

1. What is the poem about?
   Answer: Able students will say that the poem is about memories, possibly memories of people long gone from the house. The poet appears to have re-visited the house of his childhood. The house is now empty and in decline.
2. What senses does the poet appeal to in this poem?
   Answer: Students should point out that the senses the poet appeals to are:

   - Hearing – 'silence hung around like faded wallpaper'.
   - Smell – 'the smell of the past'.
   - Sight – 'yellow stains' 'light fitting' and 'floorboards'.

3. Why do you think the memories touch the poet 'with gravestone chill'?
   Answer: The memories touched the poet with 'gravestone chill' because the people, such as his parents, are possibly long dead.
4. Why do you think the poet is afraid?
   Answer: The poet could be afraid because it is as if the ghosts or spirits of the past are still in the house that they were associated with when they were alive. Or, he imagines that their spirits are still in the house.

Group/pair work (page 57)

1. What ideas of the empty house is the poet trying to create in the second line? Why is the simile appropriate?
   Answer: A possible answer could be: the house is empty.
   There used to be a number of noises and action in the house. Now the family is not living in the house and it is empty, the wallpaper has faded. The faded wallpaper and the silence

reinforce the idea that the house is deserted. As the people have faded, so has the wallpaper – which would have been renewed had there been a family living in the house.

2. List the compound words used in the poem. Why is the use of these words effective?
Answer: The compound words used are: 'gossamer-thin', which suggest the cobwebs are see through and 'ghost-like'; 'long-dim', reinforces the fact that the house has been empty for a long time.

The sinking of the SS *Golden Gate* (page 64)

1. How do we know life was dangerous in America in 1862?
Answer: Life was dangerous in America in 1862 because of the Civil War.
2. What does the captain order when he realizes the SS *Golden Gate* is on fire? Do you think his orders were sensible?
Answer: He ordered the ship to make a dash for the shoreline. The order was not sensible because when the ship picked up speed it made the fire spread.
3. George's uncle urged the Fulton boys to jump into the water. From your reading of the whole passage, was this a sensible idea?
Answer: The idea was possibly not a good one for the Fulton boys as one drowned and the other was lucky to survive. On the other hand, if they were steerage passengers, only 33 out of 134 survived. George's uncle must have died, as George went to live with another uncle after his ordeal.
4. Why do you think the men took George with them rather than the sack of potatoes?
Answer: The men probably took George with them as he was a young boy and he would have died if left on his own.
5. Why do you think most of the steerage passengers drowned?
Answer: The rich passengers who paid the most fare were probably given the first chance to go onto the lifeboats. When the lifeboats were released, panic probably set in and the passengers and crew did not wait to fill them.
6. Can you see any irony in the sinking of the SS *Golden Gate?*
Answer: People were trying to save their lives by fleeing from the American Civil War. They died anyway!

Foxes (page 67)

1. Where are foxes most likely to be found?
Answer: Foxes are most likely to be found in cities, towns,

woods, forests and rural areas. (Or, foxes can live almost anywhere.)

2. What food are foxes most likely to eat?
   Answer: Foxes are most likely to eat chickens, voles, rabbits, beetles, crabs and dead fish or seabirds.
3. What name is given to a female fox?
   Answer: A female fox is called a vixen.
4. What are foxes able to do that dogs or wolves cannot do?
   Answer: Foxes are able to climb.
5. If foxes have food left over, what do they do with it?
   Answer: Foxes will bury their food and come back to it when they are hungry.
6. What do the Japanese think about foxes?
   Answer: The Japanese believe the fox is a sacred animal.
7. Why are foxes like cats?
   Answer: Foxes have cat-like eyes and retractable claws. They also play with their pray.
8. What is interesting about the Fennec fox?
   Answer: The Fennec fox is the smallest fox. It can also hear its pray move underground.
9. Which continent has no foxes?
   Answer: Antarctica is the only continent without foxes.

Silvershine (page 69)

The captain's log: four facts:

- The sky was very blue/fluffy white clouds.
- The mountain tops are tipped with silver.
- Small strange plants are among the green grass.
- Tall silver trees are strewn with fruit as big as melons.

(Please allow valid alternatives.)

Woman in White (page 88)

- Where does Pesca come from?
  Answer: Pesca comes from Italy.
- What does Pesca look like?
  Answer: Pesca is very small, almost a dwarf.
- How does Pesca try to become an Englishman?
  Answer: Pesca tries to become an Englishman by joining in all the sports that Englishmen do. He also wears typically English outfits, including gaiters and a white hat.
- What happened to Pesca at Brighton?
  Answer: Pesca almost drowned because he could not swim.

Computer Nerd (page 92)

- What adjective is used to describe the dungeon master? Can you think of more effective adjectives to describe him?
Answer: Ugly. Students may come up with powerful, dangerous or big to describe the dungeon master. Allow any reasonable answer.
- Do you think the computer nerd is a boy or a girl? Give reasons for your answer.
Answer: Most students will think the computer nerd is a boy because boys play the sort of games described. However, if a valid case can be made for the nerd being a girl, allow it! Perhaps someone in the group will challenge stereotypes.
- What six different games does the computer nerd play?
Answer: The computer nerd plays aliens, quests, dungeon master questions, football, theme parks and intergalactic wars.

Juliet's Lament (page 96)

- What ideas are mentioned in the monologue that do not appear in the play?
Answer: Falling in love with the dangerous one (only implied in the play). A woman will never love the safe one (implied in the play, as she does not marry County Paris). Juliet mentions women in general in the monologue. Juliet compares herself with Eve.

Macbeth's Lament (page 98)

- Re-read the monologue and list Macbeth's regrets.
Answer: The students should come up with some or all of the following:
  - Having burning ambition.
  - Lost best friend when he had Banquo murdered.
  - Lost his wife's love and later her sanity.
  - Lost dignity and self-respect.

Questions on *Macbeth* (page 101)

- Macbeth 'burns' in desire to question the witches further. What does this tell us about his character?
Answer: The fact that Macbeth 'burns' in desire tells us that he is ambitious. He knows the witches are evil but still wishes to question them.
- How do we know the witches are not mortal?
Answer: We know the witches are not mortal because they talk of the supernatural things they have done when they

meet on the blasted heath (Scene 3). Also, the witches vanish after speaking to Macbeth and Banquo.

(Expect the students to use short quotes to back-up these ideas.)

- What truthful statements have the witches told Macbeth?
  Answer: The witches have told Macbeth that he is Thane of Glamis and Thane of Cawdor. The first has already happened by his father's death and the second is about to occur, when Cawdor is killed as a traitor.
  (The students need to back-up this answer by use of short quotes.)

- How do these truths lead Macbeth into harm?
  Answer: Macbeth believes the witches when they tell him that he 'shalt be king hereafter' because the second statement (Thane of Cawdor) came true.

- Why does Macbeth tell his wife exactly what happened on the heath?
  Answer: Macbeth told his wife exactly what happened on the heath because, at this point in the play, he shares everything with her as they have a good relationship.

- How does Macbeth change towards his wife after he becomes king?
  Answer: Macbeth fails to tell his wife his future plans. She did not know that he intended to murder Banquo.

- What are Lady Macbeth's worries about her husband in Act 1: Scene 5?
  Answer: Lady Macbeth believes her husband is 'too full o' th' milk of human kindness to catch the nearest way'. She does not believe he will kill King Duncan.

- What does she mean by 'catch the nearest way'?
  Answer: Lady Macbeth means that to become king, Macbeth needs to kill Duncan.

- How does Lady Macbeth intend to persuade Macbeth to kill Duncan in Act 1: Scene 5?
  Answer: Lady Macbeth intends to persuade Macbeth by pouring evil spirits in his ear – whispering to him that he could be king. She also intends to 'chastise with the valour' of her tongue. She will nag him until he is persuaded to kill Duncan.

- How does Lady Macbeth intend to change and what happens to her later to suggest the change was only for a short period of time?
  Answer: Lady Macbeth intended to change by calling on evil spirits to make her more man-like. She wishes to become hard and cruel. She does not want to be full of regrets. She does change, but the change is not lasting. Eventually, she goes mad and commits suicide.

Macbeth's speech, Act 1: Scene 7 (page 103)

- What is Macbeth's first concern after killing Duncan?
  Answer: Macbeth is concerned that he will be judged in the afterlife.
- What is Macbeth's second concern? What does he mean by a 'poison'd chalice'?
  Answer: Macbeth is concerned that he will teach 'bloody instructions' and others will copy him. In other words, somebody might murder him when he is king. Becoming king would, therefore, be a poisoned chalice.
- What sort of king does Macbeth feel Duncan has become? Does he think Duncan is a good or bad king?
  Answer: Duncan has been 'clear in his great office' – which indicates that Macbeth thinks Duncan is a good king.
- What is Macbeth's only reason for killing Duncan?
  Answer: 'Vaulting ambition' is Macbeth's only reason for killing King Duncan.
- How does Macbeth's thoughts on Duncan's kingship contrast with Macduff's desire to kill Macbeth later in the play?
  Answer: Macduff describes Macbeth as a 'hell-hound'. Macbeth also became a curse on Scotland. Macbeth was a tyrant and a bad king, in contrast with Duncan.

Sinister Monologue (page 105)

- Looking at the first 13 lines, what are the differences between what Cheryl says as she leaves the party and what she is really thinking?
  Answer: Cheryl tells her friends that she has had a great time. She goes on to say that she enjoyed the food, wine and music. In reality, she thought those at the party were a 'loony bunch'. She did not like the choice of food or music.
- At what point does the mood and atmosphere first change?
  Answer: The mood and atmosphere change by the time Cheryl starts walking. She is realistic, even pessimistic, about the party. She questions the motives of the boy 'with the greasy hair'.
- How would you evoke mood and atmosphere? Would you create mood by playing background music at various points, for example? If so, when?
  Answer: The students will possibly suggest music they know. They might suggest props. There really is no right or wrong answer for this question.

The other four questions are also open to an interesting discussion. You might suggest ideas to the groups, such as can Cheryl be persuaded to leave the house again? Ask the students to suggest reasonable punishments for Vince that are appropriate to twenty-first century Britain. Avoid ideas such as hanging, flogging, lynching and castrating!

Trapped (page 133)

1. What three things did Wayne have in his pocket?
   Answer: Wayne had a one-pound coin, an old apple core and an elastic band in his pocket.
2. What did Wayne dislike about the old man?
   Answer: Wayne did not like the old man's laugh.
3. What does the machine do?
   Answer: The machine takes people to different worlds.
4. What does the old man look like?
   Answer: The old man looks thin. He has a large, brown hat and a short, white beard.
5. What do you think will happen next?
   Answer: Most students will think either the old man has tricked Wayne and Andrew out of their money, or the boys will go to a different world and have a dangerous adventure.

Sentences (page 135)

The correct sentences are:

- Wayne checked in his pockets.
- The machine was like a spaceship.
- The old man laughed.

Jumbled sentences (page 135)

The correct sentences should read:

- I liked the story because it was scary.
- Wayne was not very brave.
- Andrew was the bravest boy in the story.
- The old man wore funny clothes.
- The machine takes you to different worlds.
- I would not step inside the machine.

The Attic (page 136)

- How does the start of the story introduce us to the idea that this could be a ghost story?
  Answer: The attic is a gloomy place. There are strange shadows lurking in dark corners.

- What new information do we glean from the second paragraph?

Answer: The new information we glean from the second paragraph is that mum wanted to turn the old attic into an art studio. She felt that the past was the past.

- How does the third paragraph create suspense?
  Answer: Most students would pick up that the rain was a pathetic fallacy. The house shaking like an old man 'burdened with some deep grief' would suggest the very house empathized with the old man, whose possessions are being thrown out. Then the suspense is increased when Harry hears the ghostly voice.

- Is the final paragraph a surprise?
  Answer: Most students would write that the final paragraph is not a surprise because we are led to believe the story would be a ghost story because of what has gone before.

Plurals not apostrophes (page 144)

Below are the correct sentences.

- The cow's calf had disappeared.
- Grandma's car was stolen.
- Pete's mate caught a giant fish.
- Oliver Gate's new book sold well.
- Her friend's cat had kittens.

The Lake Isle of Innisfree (page 145)

I will arise and go now, and go to *Innisfree*,
And a small cabin build there, of clay and wattles *made*.
Nine bean-rows will I have there, a hive for the honey-*bee*;
And live alone in the bee-loud *glade*.

And I shall have some peace there, for peace comes dropping *slow*,
Dropping from the veils of the morning to where the cricket *sings*.
There midnight's all a glimmer, and noon a purple *glow*,
And evening full of the linnet's *wings*.

I will arise and go now, for always night and *day*
I hear lake water lapping with low sounds by the *shore*;
While I stand on the roadway, or on the pavements *grey*,
I hear it in the deep heart's *core*.

Conclusion

My hope is that having read this book and used some of the material in it, you will feel that you are a much more confident English teacher. However, it is still a good idea to do a 'health check' to see where you are at. Start by asking yourself the following questions:

- Is my English classroom a place where there is a climate full of purpose and are my lessons task driven and relaxed in an academic way?
- Does my teaching have a sense of order?
- Am I supportive and helpful?
- Do my comments and feedback offer real advice and do they help students develop self-esteem and self-respect as learners?
- Are my learning activities challenging students in order that they might progress?
- Does my behaviour and my body language convey positive expectation?
- Do I care for the progress of all my students?
- Does the appearance and layout of my classroom convey a positive expectation to my students? Does it help facilitate the activities I expect my students to undertake?

To answer these questions you will need to make sure that you convey the message that student learning is of paramount importance. You can achieve this by making sure that time is never wasted. Lessons need to start promptly and you need to closely monitor student progress. Students not making progress need to be talked to in a firm but friendly manner. You need to tell them that you are not happy with their lack of progress and you need to listen to what they have to say. If there is still no progress by that particular student, you may need to involve others, such as your head of English and/or the year head. Generally, if students are not making progress in your subject the chances are that they are not making progress elsewhere. The year head will be able to monitor if the problem is across all or most subjects. Parents may need to be involved and a meeting set up. Students will, eventually, respect you for monitoring their progress. It shows them that you actually care about how they are performing in your subject.

Do take care that the work you set is appropriate for each student's ability. If a student experiences continuous failure or suffers remarks by a teacher that they are 'useless' then there will be a big negative impact on that student. The student will then give up trying or misbehave.

Misbehaviour of students may come from the fact that they have experienced continuous failure in their earlier school years, or at home. If you are able to show that you are relaxed and that you can deal with misbehaviour in a calm but firm way, students will gradually develop an interest in the learning process. This is not an easy course of action – but the rewards are great.

A classroom ethos is often built up within the first few lessons. Classrooms that establish a positive climate for learning are as follows:

- When the teacher appears more confident, warm and friendly.
- The lessons are conducted in a more business-like manner.
- Students find your lessons stimulating.
- The teacher makes good use of eye-contact.
- When there is humour in the classroom.
- Students are clear about teacher expectations and rules.
- A teacher's presence and authority are well established.

All humans, it seems, have a natural sense of curiosity. People like to develop their skills when they are engaged in various tasks. They do this for pleasure rather than as a means to an end. However, should there be a reward at the end of their hard work, they will work harder to gain the reward.

To create a climate of expectation for success, students need to be challenged – but not to the extent that they feel they will never attain what is asked of them. Work that is too easy is unrewarding, as it is too easy to achieve!

The most important factor is to support students and encourage them to learn. The teacher (you) need to convey high expectations of success. You need to be both realistic and challenging!

Students will expect you to be a good example of the expectations you wish to convey. Try not to lose your temper or employ sarcasm.

Students will find the work interesting if you show interest in the work yourself.

Using the material

I do hope that you have discovered many exciting lessons that you would wish to use with the students. I also hope you have enough information to become an effective classroom teacher. My aim is that by using this book, you will go on to another level in your English teaching. Whether you are new to English teaching, or you have been teaching the subject for some time, my aim is for you to inspire and enthuse the students so that they are able to appreciate and become proficient practitioners of English.

References

Author Unknown (undated) 'The Mermaid'.

Barton, G. (1998) *The Real World*, Heinemann.

Bayley, T.H. (1884) *The Mistletoe Bough*, available online at: www.users. dialstart.net/~2metres/poetry/ mistletoebough/mistletoebough.htm

Brontë, C. (1847) *Jane Eyre*, Smith, Elder

Brooke, R. (1914) 'Peace', Georgian Poetry, Harold Monro, available online at: http://www.warpoetry. co.uk/brooke3.html

Coleridge, S.T. (1798) *The Rime of the Ancient Mariner*, Lyrical Ballads.

Collins, W. (1860) *Woman in White*, Smith Elder.

Collins, W. (1862) *No Name*, Smith Elder.

Cookson, P. (1996) 'Let No One Steal Your Dreams', in *Hot Heads Warm Hearts Cold Streets*, J. Foster (ed.), p. 64, Stanley Thornes.

Dickens, C. (1854) *Hard Times*, Household Words.

Foster, J. (ed.) (1996) *Hot Heads Warm Hearts Cold Streets*, Stanley Thornes.

Hines, B. (1976) *Kes*, Heinemann.

Hinton, N. (1983) *Buddy*, Pearson.

Kay-Shuttleworth, J.P. (1832) 'The moral and social conditions of the working classes in Manchester 1832', available online at: http:// historyhome.co.uk/peel/p-health/ mterkay.htm

Kitchen, D. (1987) *Axed Between the Ears*, Pearson Education.

Lee, H. (1960) *To Kill a Mocking Bird*, Heinemann.

Leprince de Beaumont, J. (1748) *Beauty and the Beast*, Le Triomphe de La Verite. Publisher Unknown.

Macphail, C. (2004) *Tribes*, Puffin.

Orme, D. (1993) *Ere We Go*, Pan Macmillan.

Owen, W. (1967) 'Anthem for Doomed Youth', in *The Poems of Wilfred Owen*, Chatto and Windus.

Priestly, J.B. (1946, 1992) *An Inspector Calls*, Heineman

Prince Albert (1850) Speech at Mansion House, John Murray.

Shakespeare, W. (1951) *Macbeth*, The Alexander Text, Collins.

Steinbeck, J. (1937) *Of Mice and Men*, Heinemann.

Swindells, R. (1995) *Stone Cold*, Puffin.

Walsh, G. (1997) *The Spot on My Bum*, The King's England Press.

West, K. (2003a) *Exploring the Extreme*, Hodder & Stoughton.

West, K. (2003b) *Back to the Wild*, Nelson Thornes.

West, K. (2005a) 'Computer Nerd', in *Monologues and Duologues at*

Key Stage Three, First and Best in Education, pp. 6–8

West, K. (2005b) 'Yo Yo Kid', in *Monologues and Duologues at Key Stage Three*, First and Best in Education, pp. 9–10.

West, K. (2005c) 'Juliet's Lament', in *Monologues and Duologues at Key Stage Three*, First and Best in Education, pp. 24–25

West, K. (2005d) 'Macbeth's Lament', in *Monologues and Duologues at*

Key Stage Three, First and Best in Education, pp. 30–32.

West, K. (2005e) 'Sinister Monologue', in *Monologues and Duologues at Key Stage Three*, First and Best in Education, pp. 10–11

West, R. (2010a) 'Firework', unpublished.

West. R. (2010b) 'Water', unpublished.

Yeats, W.B. (1893) 'Lake Isle of Innisfree', A.P. Watt Ltd.

Index